Madeline Bosio

HUMAN GROWTH AND NEUROSIS
FOR RESEARCHERS, PRACTITIONERS, PARENTS
AND READERS

PERSON CENTRED THERAPY AND RESILIENCE

YOU SHALL THANK YOUR ENEMIES AND LOVE YOUR STORY

Looking into reality with eyes of wisdom

Madeline Bosio

How to heal wounds, sorrows, voids and fears of life

You shall thank your enemies and love your story

Don't walk in front of me
I may not follow
Don't walk behind me
I may not lead
Just walk beside me
and be my friend

Contents

You shall thank your enemies and love your story

Introduction

This is a letter from a client to a friend.

Dear Albert,

I gleaned some information from books as regards phenomenal or existential psychotherapy, but did not collect more than what I already knew. It is mainly about history, whereas it would (maybe) be nice to find writings by somebody who has gone through the experience of psychotherapy. It would be interesting to search out what they might have in common with each other beyond their personal history. I shall therefore try to jot down some notes, starting from me, but I think, apart from me.

There are no certainties, except one's own being. Of one's "Being" in this world.

It happens that others, though without bad intentions, deprive us, or deny us our being, our Personal Being in this world, or part of it. This causes us suffering (sometimes insanity), because after all, our aim is to exist in our personal authenticity, an authenticity that others do not always like. Sometimes the belittlement, or refusal to recognize us, (me) is so harsh that we risk losing ourselves, losing our precious, unique identity.

The aim of this kind of therapy is not to get us to win against others, which would mean getting us to win according to dominating/social rules. No… its aim is to be our companion in the voyage, "on the road" to the discovery, or the "re-discovery" of ourselves, our authenticity, even though it might be frightening, or prove to be disturbing for someone else. It is also a voyage into pain:

the pain for what we were deprived of. We may happen to love the ones who denied us recognition of our identity; and we might even happen to understand, besides our own pain, the pain and fear of others. (For example our parents)…

It is a voyage where we are simply in the company of someone who already knows it: a therapist. A person who has no intention of taking our place, or giving us his/her values, vision of the world or contents.

It is a psychotherapy of total and utmost respect for our identity, however fragile and frightening it may be.

It is a psychotherapy of respect for our fears and defences, because defences are sacred as long as we feel we are in need of them.

Psychotherapy helps to find the feelings that "had stopped" feeling. Such feelings found a refuge in a small hidden corner of the Self, since that corner was the last space left to their (my) identity.

Nobody, in this psychotherapy, wants to destroy that corner of yours, or pull you out based on their personal evaluations or opinions. You are the one who will decide, if you can manage to emerge from the corner to move towards more airy spaces. However, you can stay there as long as you deem it necessary, since that corner, however stifling and alienating it might be, is your life, your survival with all **"its good reasons"**.

For these reasons, psychotherapy does not speed up the time, but stays attuned to your rhythms. No forced "interpretations", of dreams or of anything else. No analyzing, no advice, no promises, only the silence to hear more clearly the voice (sometimes so feeble) coming from you.

No claim to change the world. Only the help that allows you to find what you are, bit by bit, and carry with you the baggage of your past.

These are a few notes, as far as I can sum it up at present.

CHIARA

When I read this letter written from a client of mine, it came to my mind the urge to gather my notes from a lifetime devoted to the discovery of psychotherapy, in order to give a reason to all the fatigue and the great amount of pain experienced by my clients' side.

These notes are intended to bear witness to how long and slow is the journey for change. A journey I shall try to describe.

The technique of the non-directive approach used in Rogerian Client-Centred Therapy, has the peculiarity of "focusing" the process flowing along the pathway taken by the client. It is a particular pathway, individual and unique, since, according to his/her own "way of being", each person will choose the therapeutic process, the form (mental, or emotional, or hallucinated), and the starting point itself.

The therapist's task is to stay in empathy. Staying with a facilitating attitude. Staying with the client. Staying with the client's Frame of Reference. Staying at the person's rhythm. Staying with unconditional positive regard. In utmost respect.

The foundations of the Rogerian Approach are in accordance with concepts and principles of existential philosophy, differing from structural theories of the Freudian and Behaviourist schools of thought, rooted in positivist philosophy. Research carried out by humanistic schools pertain to the world of "natural sciences". The phenomenal world, in opposition to structural science models, explains the "subjectivity" of the single person. Rogers directed his thought, and thus his research, to attitude rather than to technical aspects, highlighting "meaning" instead of a "therapeutic technique".

Though differing in their own subjectivity, all human beings hold universal values within themselves, "cosmic" values I would say, that inevitably link us to each other in a symphony of respect and harmony. These values are shared in philosophy, psychology, physics, biology, physiology, and religion.

Last but not least, neuroscience has scientifically proved that every behavior is linked to a feeling, to an emotion.

Going back to this work, developmental theory refers to Maslow and Piaget: all children claim the same primary basic needs. The healing process is in line with Alice Miller's theory of loss and mourning, but instead of the anger mentioned by Miller, the process relies on aspects concerning void, pain and sorrow, dreams built up in vain, (empty dreams) fear, loneliness and impotence. The "roots" of the structure (existence) are the "I-Me" and not the "I-You".

The validity of the "theory" that can be seen between the lines of the process or the pathway, relies upon CHANGE in the person. At present, it has no scientific support if not the writings of my clients, who went through this process and to whom I owe most of my notes. This means that the work comes from an experiential ground more than theoretical reading. The letter to Alberto was given to me by Chiara. It is not part of my work to ask clients to write.

My gratitude and great praise go to people who with courage and perseverance **"walked the road of their history"**. I only hope that those clients, who were psychologists, will pick up their experience with me and, since they are young, might be able to carry on the work and seek to give a more scientific contribution to the whole…

"VELVET CHAINS ARE THE MOST DIFFICULT TO CUT"

(George De Rita)

Carl Rogers and me

Carl Rogers and I were walking out of the hall after a lecture of his when he asked, "Well Madeline, who or how is a therapist?"… In a split second, I thought back to his lecture, but the answer came from inside of me: "Being myself and my feelings". "Right!" he answered. The answer surely came from what I had just heard and experienced at his lesson.

Time proved it…

It is being myself together with the client's "frame of reference". Being with his feelings and my empathy. Being with his words and felt meanings. Being with his life history and my knowing what should have been for the growing child. Being with the voids of what was not. Being with telling, reading "subjective" reality. Being with wounds caused by careless caregivers. Being with fear and sometimes, terror for what was happening and being without protection … left alone in a world "wild and unknown".

When I started working as a therapist, my main struggle consisted of "having faith" in what Rogers states: *keep with the client wherever he/she goes; however one is, whatever one says. Just follow the flowing of the stream and he/she will lead you to the right places to be explored". Trust their power. Trust their actualizing tendency. It is "there" where you need to use the "tools of life". Life in the sense of an "organismic being".*

The journey shows that, on one hand there is the client's reality, on the other hand, there is what "could or should have been". It is a help to "work out" what has been, a help to "work on" how he/she felt.

Working on one's life: present and past – on when one built "craving dreams" trying to attain what was authentically needed for healthy growth. Seeking together for what happened: what made him/her turn into a suffering being owing to streams of pain, disappointments, frustrations, fears and punishments for not being what the adult wanted or, owing to what the adult regrettably felt towards the child during the age of psychological and affective development.

The reason for some ways of being lies in the feelings caregivers had toward their children, causing them to behave in ways that were harmful for the growth of the organism.

Years of working like this, gave me the opportunity to experience the fact that "theory" is inside each person and belongs to "that" single life and it is from in there, that the person can come out and turn into what they really feel they are. There will be harmony with themselves and with the worlds of other "beings".

Science needs explanations and proof. For the time being, I have only the testimony of my clients, some letters they wrote spontaneously and some metaphors I use. I just hope that these can be the dwellings for future theory.

What is the main "work" for a therapist? The fundamental element is to stay with the client at whatever level one wants or needs to stay and "explore" that piece of world. There is always "a reason" why the person is "there". That present way of being actually corresponds to what Rogers calls "the good reason". It is "a piece of history", a distortion of the actualizing tendency. Inside each of us there is a developmental organismic pattern according to our needs, to our growing self, to our interaction with the world outside, that should be satisfied. However, most times, it is distorted.

In my experience, I have noticed that some people do not want to know what happened, to discover the reasons they are suffering, but they just want to feel better. That is okay. Cognitive therapy can work for them. Others want to go deep inside to understand what is going on and thus change certain ways of being. In this case, it is necessary to go back, get in touch and identify the feelings, VOIDS, pains left behind because they are too heavy to bear. Realities are too incomprehensible and feelings too challenging for the growing child to cope with. The Person-Centred Approach works mainly on feelings and is highly successful.

Rogers gave me the tools to get here. I shall tell you what I found…
I CAN HELP YOU SEE WHAT HAPPENS
I CAN HELP YOU SEE HOW IT HAPPENS
I CANNOT SHOW YOU THE WAY
IT IS YOUR WAY
I CAN STAY STILL OR WALK WITH YOU
SIDE BY SIDE IN YOUR PHENOMENICAL WORLD

My thanks to George De Rita:
Words are too empty to translate what
I feel for you. For a teacher and friend.
For the hours shared together in Rome.
Later in Milan, working together
In Bologna.
For the days when my experiences,
with your help, went deep into
my soul and into my memories…
To You George

The dawn of humanistic psychotherapy

I shall point out a few basic assumptions of the humanistic orientation in psychotherapy. Evidence is for the main characteristics distinguishing the Humanistic Approach, which has to do with the person's experiential world. No theory can be used to work on people's phenomenal world, which is "subjective" and thus unique.

It is subjective in the sense that "my" relationship with my parents first, with the outside world later, my interactions with cultural, social, moral rules and principles are perceived and interiorized according to my "developing way of being" which is unique. I am "Single" in a world of "Many".

Humanistic psychology contains a physiological as well as an ethical vision of the person, thus, of the world, with its roots in Existential Philosophy. Human contact is of such a special nature that we must revise many psychological problems. In order to build a psychological model, researchers have made use of basic concepts: sensations, perceptions, representations, ideas, feelings, emotions, needs, desires and so on.

However, there are "moods" that do not fit into this picture. Their outlines are "evanescent" and not easy to grasp. Some even seem to dissolve if we try to touch them. The "Ego" is not very assertive and seems to stay "on the outskirts". One finds oneself on the "threshold of nothingness", but cannot deny their existence. The Ego in torment seems to find a safe place there, like a dock or an oasis. There, one can forget oneself. Nevertheless, this nothingness comes from "human contact", which is in communion with the universe, for which we are made. Thus, human life is not made only of dates, periods, events that determine/design our lives. Our biography cannot tell everything. Only facts, translated into words, can tell the story and share it with another person. The Ego is not always present in each instant of its story and this story is not entirely made of facts. It involves, or better still, it necessarily dwells in mute zones, silent places, which, although they seem to vanish into the shadows or even into the night, are certainly more fertile than resounding, noisy places. They are unconscious zones, but on condition that this unconscious world is given the meaning it deserves.

This is the source, giving rise to the possibility of examining psychical phenomena in their essence independently from how they individually take place, classifying them, establishing significant correlations to each other. We started from a chaotic flux, and we made the effort to give this flux a form, a structure, a "frame of reference".

This philosophical and psychological introduction leads us directly to Rogers and to his "way of working and of being." Psychical disorders are due to threatening, conflictual life experiences, leading to distortion of the Self, thus a distortion from the Actualizing Tendency. The consequence is Existential disorders.

A successful psychotherapy leads the person to dig down along the pathway of past and present experiences - down to the roots of "unfinished business" (The distorted Self) - down into the inner world, healing sufferance, removing distortions. At this point of the process, there is a shift to "Humanistic Existing in the world": once we have worked and accepted our **inner limits**, we can face the "Limits of Existence": the **outer limits.** From a philosophical point of view: "our existing **in** the world".

In other words, once we have gone through the process of our inner world, the following step consists of experiencing the "existing of nothing/no sense" pertaining to our "being **in** the world". A stage of the process causing uncertainty- finitude of "being"- the end and death of all. Uncertainty dissolves, when one gains consciousness of "impermanence"; accepts the limits of being. This last step consists of "transcending" materialistic sense: the "chains of being" according to a spiritual paradigm.

It is beyond doubt that for whoever gains such consciousness, the feeling is: freedom. Living in the "here and now". ***Freedom is just another word for nothing else to lose".***

A thread of grass
and nothingness… is Nothing
A silence and
inertia… are Nothing
Nothing can be something
Something doesn't exist, because:
Nothing or the Absolute are the same thing
Being or not being in this dimension
are the same thing
Here and there are equally the same…
From: A psychotherapy? No… a lifetime (M. Bosio)

Part 1
The process in psychotherapy

I searched down into the depths of our wounds and this is what I found.
Wounds have a voice… are only waiting for somebody to tell their story.
Wounds that hath no voice in the dark of silence. Angels could help them, but…
They cannot hear… We can only appeal to the limits of our minds. A limit we cannot fathom.
But… it is that border which opens on to the infinite…

1 Actualizing tendency and distorsion of the self

"It's gonna be a long walk home"...
Bruce Springsteen

Human beings live in the world in interaction with themselves (I – Me) and interacting with the world and others (I – Thou).

From the very beginning, from birth and way up to late adolescence, this flowing of life gives rise to the structuring of one's personality. When "being" is free to express the Self, according to its actualizing tendency, a mature and authentic personality will develop.

This means that experience has responded to certain needs and desires. Needs and desires surface according to *personal and authentic* feelings and needs: one's potentialities. When needs and desires are satisfied, there is a feeling of health; *experience is positive.* Emotions nurture and give way to the construction of **trust** toward the world and **self-esteem** for oneself. **The "actualizing tendency".**

In contrast, frustrating experiences, impossibility of being oneself, uneasiness and violence suffered in relationships with those who were supposed to give support and collaboration to the growing child, will leave signs that create unsatisfied and inadequate adults. **"Distortion of the Self".**

In our *subjective* world, we perform behaviours intended to attain satisfaction of the needs and desires which are the foundations of our existing. Thus, the actualizing tendency builds our personality, but can be hindered or distorted owing to wounds and voids caused by others. For reasons explained further on, painful experiences lead us away from our contact with authentic parts of our being. In other words, we slowly **lose contact with our real self**. When we lose contact with the true self, we set up behaviours that are, most times, a product of a "distortion" of the self. It is here that a "neurotic" personality takes hold. It becomes a source of dependency, submission, domination, narcissistic ties, violence, masochism, perversion, and so on.

Why does this happen?

On one hand, the "Self" is incapable of coping "with that" reality, (we shall see this further on) on the other hand, the authentic Self "will not give up" hope to satisfy the frustrated need. Thus, all our "troubles" begin with a wound. A **wound** caused by *"what has been"* and a **void** produced, instead, by *"what has not been"*. What has not been will turn into a **"strawberry ice cream"**. We shall see this later.

"What has not been" is a *void*, a painful sorrow as regards oneself, (I-Me) when personal needs are not satisfied. "What has been", in the negative sense of experiencing, are *wounds* caused by conflicts, misunderstandings, abuse and threatening environments. (I-Thou). An "uneasy life" in adulthood, lays its foundations on the presence of our "inner child" who is claiming the *"not given"*…and on our inability to heal the **"wounds"**. In fact, the "inner child" has never given up the attempt to satisfy needs and desires… A hope, a dream in something that shall never come true: "I need your caring and sharing- I need your unconditioned positive regard and acceptance- I need your respect and love-"and so on.

The frustrating "experience" of the "not given", (voids) is burdened with the experience of "what happened" (wounds); in other words, **"what reality produced". This is where all our troubles originate**, because they are too difficult to manage and too painful to accept. *Defensive systems* are set up to control or even deny authentic feelings and emotions and to safeguard and protect against dangerous (for the Self) situations coming from the outer world. This is the neurotic structure BUILT to cover our authentic Self. So there are *"Defence mechanisms"* built to control or deny *wounds; frustrations and pains; safety distances*, and *"Behavioural Patterns"* built with the "dream" to satisfy the *"not given"*.

Defensive and behavioural patterns/strategies, will always be with us…**faithful but tyrannical**. We shall further consider this aspect below. At present, we can see that this is the structure operating in the world. We reiterate behaviours and strategies intended to satisfy our "frustrated inner child". It is important to understand that these are only "parts" of our Structure, parts causing the "neurotic way of being": we are not only "negativity", but have also "positive" ways of being.

Unfortunately, defensive mechanisms and strategies turn out to be failures in interaction with others, with things and also with ourselves. Let us just consider adolescents who self-harm in order to avoid an "emotional pain".…. *"I cut myself because physical pain is less disruptive than emotional feeling".* We generally call these "Neurotic Behaviours"

It might happen that the unprotected child *buries* all the emotional world and needs *deep inside*: the **"not me"** described by the famous psychiatrist H. Sullivan. The child rejects any kind of feelings. "Thrown out of the Self". Adults bearing such experience will be destined to "REPEAT" what happened to them. In their "inner world," no child is claiming or calling for something. There is a rejecting adult. Inside, there is only a world of darkness and silence. Adults who will refuse and ill-treat all that may remind them of what is concealed. **An ill-treating person.** In his/her "frame of reference", *love is an enemy.* Defeats and failures will be well controlled but compensated by a *harsh* (or dead) heart (character) that "does not cry".

Now, life has become a relentless organization against a *painful reality* of voids and wounds. A reality that did not find, in early childhood, the strength to exist just as it was: **"here and now".** A child who is incapable of facing or even understanding the outside reality, incapable of containing feelings. The presence of a caregiver explaining what happened, or how things were happening, would have helped the child to let *"authentic feelings and emotions"* flow, and thus **integrate** them in his "history of life", *giving them recognition,* though painful and not what the child needed.

I am referring to frustrating, painful and sometimes frightening realities or other realities too confused or distorted for a child to understand. Only the **loving arms** and words of an adult who with **empathy** shares, listens, *respects feelings* and "handles" them in a "safe way", would help the child to steadily integrate them in the stream of life. That means letting them be part of the "self".

When this does not happen, the only way to survive is to "organize oneself with *defence mechanisms and dreams.* The dream is the "promise" that sooner or later, it will be possible to attain what is desired or needed.

The Self therefore sets out to organize its life to fulfill the dream, instead of functioning in "congruency" with reality. The organism loses its capacity to function in harmony with the organizing tendency.   Now the link is with dreams, desires and defence mechanisms. The path full of behaviours "reiterating" the initial pain. Only by coming to terms with the "unfinished business" of the past, is it possible to *find the way* to walk in the *"here and now"* of the present. (Existential Concept).

The Way Out is: through, made possible only with a psychotherapy dealing with feelings and emotions. If we do not put an end to our unfinished business, that is, solve problems collected in the past, since that "past" will not stay behind us, but *will always be walking in front of us…*

The process consists of reading the present and rewriting the past, **because** in the present we **work,** or better, *struggle,* using the tools of our past. The contents are different because now we are adults, but "the game of cards" is almost the same. There are patterns set up with the intent to obtain what we need and "expect" from others. We will distinguish patterns acquired from the outside world, (cultural-social-or other) from patterns defending us from our "inner chaos"…

Therapy will guide the person to get in touch with "different" parts (or pieces) of themselves. The most important insight is **the shaping** of an **"adult"** part of the self and a **"child"** part, our "inner child". So there are two **"actors"** in this journey!

In psychotherapy the adult part is the "rational" one that tries to re-construct or re-write the story and steadily read past and present **"reality and emotions"**. The person sees and feels aspects of the present and the past story of life, made possible by means of the **frame of reference**. There are situations that need a "graft" (concept) from the therapist, in order to determine a "congruency" in the experience reported, especially in family situations where messages and reality were distorted. Let us see an example.

The therapist's graft.

Cl. *When I used to come home from kindergarten there was no lunch… my mum was always tired…*

    Th. *Mummy was tired but you didn't have your meals…*

    Cl. *Yes… that was so…*

    Th. *How do you feel about this?…*

    Cl. *…(Crying)… (Silence …)…*

    Th. *I feel it is painful for you…*

    Cl. *Yes… but mummy was very kind to me … she would comb my hair…*

    Th. *How old were you?…*

    Cl. *Three…*

    Th. *At that age a child's hair "must" be combed by an adult…*

Surprised eyes glanced back to me and sobs came surfacing.

By means of these grafts, (concepts) the **therapist restores congruency**. These are parts of the "inner child" which must be "searched for". Parts are not immediately "reached or visible", since they have been more or less carefully buried into deep folds of our being, with the attempt to store them because they are too painful or because they could cause "too much trouble". Nevertheless, the main player in our present behaviour is our childhood experience, ignored at a conscious level owing to a number of unconscious mechanisms (denial-removal-avoidance-displacement) set up to drive away from self-awareness those painful or negative feelings that, in spite of these defense mechanisms, **keep on "calling"**.

The unfolding of one's experience is not a narration in terms of topics, items or theories. When we try to represent our world, we are dealing with "broken mirrors" or pieces of a puzzle, which are lost in our memories, or in drawers full of defense mechanisms. We must remember that we are wounded and damaged "beings" and sometimes, only able to perceive "distorted fragments" of our realities.

The vision could be of a shabby house (or temple?...) we managed to build with wounds – chips of reality – dogmas – misleading statements – old "films" – small victories – sporadic revenges – people hated – people loved. We build our idea of "reality" of such inadequate materials that we need to defend it at all costs, to retain the illusion that we are succeeding in keeping it indestructible.

The paradox is that, these chips and fragments of memories are of great value. These broken pieces are indispensable in the therapeutic process. They help us to "come through" and re-build our story.

2 The pathway to becoming oneself - to resilience

As we can see, the "main actor" is the part belonging to "childhood experience", but carefully ignored at a conscious level. At the core of our behaviour, there are our needs that, when life starts out, are very few but fundamental.

** to be nurtured

** to be kept warm and dry

** to be reassured by a warming and caring presence.

As we develop, our needs and desires increase in number and complexity. Self-consciousness is steadily emerging with the aid of the outside world. We are starting to build the "I-me" and the "I-thou".

Now, let us go back to basic needs. When need springs up, something in the organism has already been stimulated: a "feeling" of the self, experiencing discomfort, owing to "the need in action". Like an engine that sends a red signal on the dashboard "asking" for the fuel tank to be filled, the infant's body is experiencing hunger and sends a signal to the world: "I need to eat". The "world outside" receives the signal and adequately satisfies the need. The desire is satisfied, the need is soothed. Suckling has a pleasant feeling. The infant has a *gratifying* thus **positive experience**. Crying was *successful:* it had a positive effect...– self-esteem – a supply of love, thus *"trust"* in the Self. As time goes by, this trust will become "trust" in others.

Lovingness the real food for life:

It is important to understand that *"lovingness"* toward a child does not mean the mere supply of food or material needs, but the caregiver's *"mood:"* the feeling, the atmosphere communicated. Food may even consist of bread and water; what deeply affects the child's experience is **"how it is given"**. A gratifying experience builds up **"good feeling bricks"** for the child's Self. The experience gives way to **a positive and trusting "way of being"**:

°°° When fruit on a tree reaches a perfect ripeness, we just touch it and it "gently drops" into our hand

°°° If fruit is not ripe, we need to "pull" it off.

°°° Ripe and left too long on the tree, it ends up all mushy in the hand.

°°° When ripe, some kinds of fruit "drop off" on their own. This is what should happen to the young of humans when "ripe"/ready to go into the world.

By contrast, it often happens that the *"stream of life"* tears a person from the tree, to be set free. This happens because on one hand, life is claiming, on the other hand there is a family that did not carry out the "job" properly for the child's growth. Rogers would say it did not **"facilitate the actualizing tendency"**. So the only way to "drop" from the tree is to "tear away"…

When behaviour is positive, the grown-up child "senses" the world is calling and, though with feelings of sadness, moves into the world. It is not a slamming of the door. No "running away from home". Instead, there will be a young person well aware of him/herself. It is life calling and it is stronger than ties with the past.

Sometimes situations cause negative experiences giving way to a "sour taste" of being. Why? … Because needs were not satisfied, experiences were painful and distorted.

An example:

A little girl says to her father, *"… I don't want you to touch me "there" anymore…stop it!"* Father answers: *"what's this? I thought you liked it!"*… Experience is very frustrating, at times painful or frightening. The child's experience is of *"pain"* for what happened, a feeling of inadequacy, uneasiness, of unlovingness.

For many years, children are unable to "point out" the caregiver's mistakes. The only explanation they have is: they are not up to their task – If they are not loved it is their fault.

Other examples:

1 – The child makes a drawing and gives it as a "present" to the caregiver: *"mummy I've drawn a nice picture for you"*. The adult looks and says, *"What is this rubbish?"*… The child did not ask you if it was nice, but only asked you to accept the gift… and the child has a feeling of failure and unlovingness…

The child's message is as follows: "I am giving you my drawing as a sign of love". The parent replies "I don't want it…"

2 – A child cries, he has fallen down and the parent spanks him. The child was not expecting a punishment, but to receive assistance and be reassured in his fright, his physical and moral pain.

3 – "Mummy I got 9/10 for my composition!" "Oh… but your sister is much better at speaking dialect.

AN INCONGRUENCY BETWEEN "WHAT" THEY DID AND "WHAT" CAME BACK

In all these situations, the child's expectations were disappointed: he feels inadequate and that it is his fault. In these cases the" bricks of experience" will be set up "inadequately" because inside they carry a feeling of low self-confidence- or carelessness – or shyness –or something distorted. The main idea steadily making way in the Self is, "something does not work…" In other words, there is **no "positive regard", no "unconditioned respect or love"**. (Rogers).

There are situations when experience is so disrupting that the "bricks" **are dumped**. It is the defensive mechanism of "not me" (H.S.Sullivan).

As I said, in these cases, the child's **experience** is *frustrating: – **needs** are not satisfied, and this opens up the **"Void"** (empty needs)*. Emptiness could be partially healed with the aid of an adult, who could help the child to "read/face reality" adequately according to the age. It is a reality that leads the child into the "realm" of others' "Frames of Reference" (Rogers), a reality that, between the lines, is **"showing the truth"**.

Let us go back to the three examples.

1 – The reality is, *mummy only wants perfect designs, as you see she needs all things to be perfect.*

2 – The reality is, *if you disobey her orders you know she gets angry, even though it may not be your fault if you fell over.*

3 – The reality is, *mummy has no interest in your marks…*

Reality explained with a caring attitude to the child, with words of respect towards the caregiver. These are the conditions of congruency, transparency and acceptance. Such conditions are hard to achieve since it is not easy to find people or caregivers able to behave with such delicacy and sensitivity.

This is what I call a **"bath in reality"**. The task consists of "holding" without judging or blaming. It is wrong when we think it is "cruel" to do this to a child. Cruelty is an experience already existing in the child. It is unhealthy to try to soften or transform that reality, or to uphold a parent. Certain psychological theories state that it is necessary to show parents as the image of perfection. I have proof through experience that a bath in reality helps to face reality: taking it as it is.

In an age of the "concrete mind", children can accept explanations more than we imagine. The point consists of "trusting" the child, and leaving the child with ***his dignity and power***. *This is lovingness and unconditional regard.*

Further, we will notice that, when families are dysfunctional, the environment is "stormy". The hard work lies in pointing out that at home there are **"bitter green apples"** and not the "sweet red apples" the child is longing for... because "that is the reality". However painful, a child can learn how to "handle" it. Little by little, with the aid of an empathic adult who, at that moment, is the child's "river-banks", where he can safely let emotions flow without the fear of being overwhelmed, thus disintegrating the Self...

This work is getting reality "into focus", experiencing it in all its congruency. Truth has never killed anyone: on the contrary, deceit can lead to dissociation. In my experience, I have noticed this "bath" in reality does not lead to hatred or aggressive attitudes toward the caregiver. Some theories state: "A parent must always be seen as invincible and never weak in order to interiorize a positive image". I do not share this statement. Experience has shown me that a child only needs **"congruency"**. An internal congruency between "inner experiencing" and what happens outside. Rightness leaves the child with personal dignity and Personal Power, giving rise to Self-esteem and respect for oneself. These feelings lead to full respect toward the "Other" and for "weak caregivers".

Unfortunately, it does not happen, so the "voids" and "wounds" of the developing child remain. The resulting frustration gives rise to defensive attitudes for the safeguard of the Self that has to face these frustrating experiences, all alone.

Example: Annie (mentioned above) was expecting approval. She needed:

** to be reinforced in her schoolwork

** to be reassured with care and attention. That is, by "sharing" her world.

** not to be neglected or denied.

** not to be ignored, thus she "exists".

** to experience the feeling of "belonging".

This did not take place. *A **Void** opens up*. The answer that *wounded* her heart was worse: no lovingness, no hopes. The frustrating experience was buried by the defense mechanism of "removal". (In Annie's case). The unsatisfied desire/need will start weaving the "Dream". This path leads to become **a "slave" of the dream** that turns into a "strawberry ice cream". We shall see how it works.

How did Annie grow up?

Annie's relationship with her parents was painful and frustrating. Her mother's attitudes were of denigration and devaluation. Her father always pushed her toward high goals. Her trophies were "his glory" in social life. The girl collected prizes in many fields: study, sport, her profession.

Annie has grown into a skillful, clever professional, but gets into relationships that are painful failures. She is always "used" for her intelligence and cleverness, cheated out of her intuitions and eventually rejected. As regards her romantic life, she relies upon her cleverness in an attempt to "win" a place beside her "prince". When they understand they can "use" her intelligence, they turn mean. Afraid of losing them, she gets more intimate and closer. Their reaction is rejecting and cold and they drop her. In other circumstances she can no longer bear their uncaring and extremely narcissistic attitudes, thus, puts an end to the relationship.

Explaining these dynamics is complicated, but it is easy to understand that the outcome has to do with **patterns and dreams *"that will come true"*, built up during Annie's childhood.**

In spite of everything, we must bear in mind that:

1. Defensive mechanisms are veils lowered over our wounds and painful realities: the disdainful mother and narcissistic father(Annie's parents)

2. A child presents elements suitable for "working on dreams": illusion, magic idea, omnipotent power that turn out to be failures.

How can we explain this?

A child's psychical structure is the following:

** ILLUSION. Whatever is sought, does "exist."

** MAGIC IDEA. Get what you desire.

** OMNIPOTENT POWER. The attempt to get what is desired has no limits.

** CREATIVENESS. A child's creative thought is boundless.

** PRINCIPLE OF DESIRE. Reality corresponds to the inner world. Reality of the outside world made up of renunciation, sacrifice, limits, is non-existent. "Whatever I desire, I shall have it at once".

** INNOCENCE. The child looks into the world with eyes of innocence.

A frustrating experience can interrupt the development of these aspects, causing distorted behaviours. We shall see this aspect later.

As the child grows up, other personality structures develop: at the age of eleven or twelve, intelligence develops in hypothetic-deductive reasoning. The Principle of Pleasure still dominates the sense of "limits" that is coming to consciousness. Experiences unfold. Here we are dealing with frustrated experiences so in this case, along with the "growing up," there is the concealed "unsatisfied child" (the inner child). Behavioural patterns/strategies of the past keep on working, in the attempt to satisfy our infant needs.

Let us summarize these aspects

So far, we see that adults behave according to childhood patterns. The adult says to the inner-child "don't worry, now I shall go into the world and obtain the "not given"… Alas, something does not work and one repeats an endless story. The reason why this is dysfunctional is explored below.

Nevertheless, there is a "functioning Self" and "being in the world" is possible, because besides frustrating experiences, the person will also have positive experiences and feelings. The negative experiences of the past are "covered" by defensive mechanisms. Should this fail, the person goes towards psychiatric behaviours. As long as we function within a certain harmony and a certain amount of pain and frustrations, we are able to live a decent life.

When life becomes too painful to cope with, owing to our defensive mechanisms that turn out to be too disruptive in our existence, the only way out is to go through our past story for a psychotherapy. It is a work of slow and painful reading of the present and past realities. Once we gain the capacity to **accept REALITY** for what it has been and are able to **"give funerals"** to our desires and let go of our dreams, we shall **recover the "actualizing tendency"** that we were denied.

The stream of life will move along one of the fundamental principles for our psychical system: the **Principle of Reality**. It is the principle that develops out of the previous "childish" Principle of Pleasure. By accepting reality, we accept the **"limits"** of life and the limits collected in our past "story". We relinquish "omnipotence" and accept our **impotence.** When we say farewell to our "dreams" (they were **empty dreams**…) and mourn their loss, we are giving up the need. At this point, we face reality, and look at the world, just as it is.

By means of this long process, which is a "dying to oneself" in order to "rise again", what have we changed?

** The sense of omnipotence gives way to a more genuine sense of the Limit of things (this will match a philosophical principle) and the acceptance of impotence.

** Instead of the principle of desire/pleasure, there will be the rule of the Principle of Reality.

** The dream turns into the Reality of the Present curtailed by the reality of the past.

** The magic attitude turns into Wisdom

** The *Creative Part* remains and the "inner child" carries it with itself for integration with the adult part.

** During the search for oneself and for the lost (hidden) parts, there is a work of reinforcement of our "foundations" consisting of an **increase in Self-Esteem and in restoring our dignity.** Esteem and dignity that *spring from love and self-respect.*

** It is this "restored" part that will "go back" and fetch the infant part, that is, the "inner child" who bears one's **"essence".**

This last step will be, when we stop "dragging" our little child around the world, seeking someone who will satisfy our Dreams (needs). Dreams that nobody will ever satisfy…

** In the end, it will be the adult within us, who, having worked through the therapeutic process "takes care of the little child". Here we are in line with an existential principle: **"the two ends have met and together, shall flow toward the ocean of life…" (Carl Rogers).**

** The two ends are **"original wounds"** that are now healed, and **"funeral of dreams"** which means accepting the void.

DO NOT SMILE

Oh! I pray you my dear child
do not smile, no do not smile, I pray you.
Oh! do not smile any longer my little girl
I pray you…
Do no longer hide, my child
your sorrow, your shame
innocent
behind your beautiful smile.
The lords of power
are not worthy
of your sweet smile.
come, I shall take you far away with me
where you shall be able to laugh and laugh
in the wind of freedom
that shall never hurt you.

The story of Narcissus… a lonely boy

Narcissus is a lonely child. He always strived to "be seen", to receive consideration, but his caregivers, involved in things of life, were always too distant or engaged to notice him; to lovingly share some time with him. When they did so, and it was very seldom, they were always in a hurry and their attitude was usually cold and distant. Empathy and unconditional positive regard were lacking. Thus, Narcissus decided to give himself love; on his own (to fix things as best he could). So he makes a new game in which he is himself and at the same time, the "other" from him. In this way, he believes he can give himself what others are not giving. He says to himself "Oh! you are a "beautiful" boy, the "best", the "cleverest", the most "popular", everybody "loves you"… and so on.

Children have a magic thought and are sure that soon or later they will succeed in getting what they need. Narcissus stores this magic thought and builds a Dream: "one day, mummy and daddy or later on when I'm big, someone else will notice me, and appreciate me, and really love me…"

Time goes by and Narcissus grows into a handsome lad. One day, while walking in a park, he comes across a pond. Standing on the edge, he sees a face looking at him… so he gets nearer, with curiosity. He notices that the other one is curious too. He smiles and sees a smile coming back to him. At this point he remembers **the dream** and thinks that finally his glorious day has arrived. **HIS HOPES** are about to turn into reality. He thinks: "…somebody is finally noticing me… so it's true…now he will appreciate me… we will be friends".

Blinded with the eagerness to realize his dream, Narcissus does not notice that it is always himself; only himself reflected in the water and while he leans over to embrace the nice person facing him, who is spreading out his arms, looking so happy about meeting him, he falls into the pond and drowns.

Since he never had someone acting as a "mirror" to him, thus fostering the experience of recognizing himself by distinguishing the "other from him", Narcissus is not able to recognize himself in the water. Lost in his dream, prisoner of his defensive mechanisms and of the narcissistic patterns adopted, he is not able to realize what is going to happen, and happy in his illusion, he loses his life. **"In the wounds there is what you did to me…"**

The Narcissus of this book does not die…

When he grows up, the characters he created in his mind, by means of his fantasy and magic thought, are now *"Life on the stage"*. The stage is for him, like a drug. He needs it like the air he breathes.

In psychotherapy, if he should work out the mourning we were talking about, the first anguish that would surface, would sound as follows: "…*but …if I give up being on the stage, there is nothing else… I see a great void…*". For Narcissus the most difficult step to overcome is not the empty stage. It is "no stage, **no applauses",** the precious element that feeds his "need for appreciation and love"… The void is the "empty space" that opens up when what you need in childhood is not satisfied/given. A void that we always manage to fill up with a "surrogate" (stage and applause) and when empty, it starts howling. As a client says, *"It is silence screaming"*…

The "sorrow" Narcissus is suffering from, is not the pain of his "history" **(it is denied),** but still has to do with his "strategies". This is explained below.

Nevertheless, Narcissus has a "very good reason" to use a "strategy". The feeling of emptiness and nothingness appears when the stage is empty. If we stay with his "frame of reference," there is congruency, because it is through "others" that he "shines". The only way for him to exist, is to shine, noticed, loved....

Therapist to Narcissus: *If you shine of your own light, the void would not come along when you are alone...*

Narcissus: *Oh!...No! I cannot shine with my own light...because I would be ALONE... no...no.*

Therapist: *...This is the price of freedom...But you are not alone ... once you are free...there are many other suns like you shining with their own lights...you are constellations of light!!.*

Narcissus: *But I cannot fathom being without a stage... and an audience.*

Narcissus has his good reasons to say this... Why? Because it is the stage, the audience that are **"working"** as a lid **to cover** and conceal his sorrow, his wounds, his loneliness which are, the **real /true VOID. His true experience is of** the **"Not given"**, the "carelessness" of careless hands, and **"Wounds"**, rejecting interactions. He would indeed be in anguish should he be alone, because that "being alone" is **not** of a person who has cut the threads with his past; thus becoming self-sufficient. It is **the** "starving/craving for the stage lights". The true "being alone" of Narcissus is "I am not considered. I am alone in this world. I am a lonely boy... I am scared". (No external, thus internal Landmarks).

It is not easy to be perfect caregivers, but let us try to understand where the first troubles originate. Let us go back to the example of the "hungry child". When an infant is hungry, he sends a message to the world "using" his cry, the only means of communication at his disposal. The adult responds according to feelings stimulated or aroused by such call. The following is from a therapeutic session:

Grace

Little Marc is hungry, he cries. His mother receives the message and *reacts in keeping with feelings of her past and present story.* The experience of her own story will strike certain cords and not others.

Marc's mother had read many books about looking after infants. The cords that vibrated in her world of emotions when Marc cried in hunger were not about Marc's need and her response to him. *"What is happening? What does the book say about these strange/angry feelings?"* Feelings and emotions that welled up were coming from her story and some "unfinished business" having to do with **"Power"**... No lovingness at all...

Grace read the baby's call as an "overbearing message". **"He is bossing me. He wants me there at his beck and call"**. For others the cry might cause a feeling of annoyance, or fear. Obviously. The "sanest" is of lovingness and care...but it does not always go that way...

In our case, Grace experienced a feeling of hatred and rage. These feelings brought up the fear of having to yield to the "little tyrant" who is calling and stealing her time. For her it is a challenge, not a needy child. She does not want to be a loser... Unfortunately, infants, bestowed with a deep empathic sensibility, feel the rejection by means of various communication channels: voice, the kind of perspiration, the pressure on their skin, the atmosphere in the family, the adult's temper (Harry. S Sullivan). In our case, Marc has an experience of rejection, frustration and impotence owing to his state of total dependence. The baby will experience a feeling of terror for his survival. He feels he is in danger and unable to solve the problem. The feeling of discomfort is recorded. The immediate reaction is of screaming, agitation and refusal to be fed. When the crying goes on for a long time, there is a biological defensive mechanism: the child falls into a deep sleep... anaclitic depression.

Studies carried out in orphan-asylums where children are often left alone, have proved these reactions.

Our Narcissus has grown up... and his defensive mechanism is:... "Nobody cares for me... Ok... then I myself shall manage to get myself seen...."Unfortunately, should he gain visibility and maybe success, it will be a "bottomless pitl". We shall understand this further.

The modern-day Narcissus: The illusory nature of virtual reality

I would like to jot down a few considerations about the current identity of Narcissus and, of course, about the ways in which narcissism manifests itself.

It has become noticeable over the past few years of this cultural and historical period that identity "appears" ever more frequently via expressive media and technologies. A new breed of Narcissus is developing at breakneck speed. He does not "appear", but increasingly cloaks himself in technical means of identity creation. Often, we are dealing with a Narcissus who tries to fill his own emptiness and solitude with substitute objects such as tablets, smartphones and video games. His "individualism" goes beyond seeking the approval of an "audience"; it escalates into a virtual contest, using means that are characteristic of psychosis and finally of autism.

Narcissism ends up burning itself out in a sort of autistic short circuit, without even finding an opportunity for communication (futile in any case because without an objective, but useful as an exchange with another-albeit superfluous –person), and then concludes its trajectory "in the world" at the extreme end of virtual affirmation of loss, with the risk of a suicidal gesture as its only outcome.

In other words, unlike classic narcissism, where spectators are made of flesh and blood, and it is possible to keep loneliness and sense of emptiness at bay through human relationships, in virtual narcissism the audience is (virtual) megabytes. Success does not involve human contact but is achieved via "likes" so that loneliness and inner void become an abyss, taking the adolescent to the brink of dissociation.

The outcome being sought is not success in defeating the "other than self", rather all is played out in the extreme defeat of the Self (in real life), so that the effect burns itself out because it implodes. The new addictions can be seen in this light: – addiction to technology and the resulting syndromes, such as *hikikomori* (literally, "pulling inward, self-isolation"). We are witnessing a Narcissus who, in the quest for affirmation, has exploded with the deadly weapon of addiction to tablets, video games and social networks.

This is the pathway taken by lethal narcissism, in which one becomes famous by dying. At the clinical level, one could say that an adolescent decides subconsciously to die in order to be seen. Why does this occur?

The roots of such unhappy circumstances are once again found, as might be expected, in relation to developmental dynamics (and thus, also possible regression) in the pathology of the caregivers of these poor creatures. It is truly disheartening to observe how young people are immersed in the "superficial way of being" of adults, which are just as intolerable as the resounding echo of their indifference, masked by sham attentiveness that amounts to control, serving the parents' peace of mind as opposed to a sincere interest in the child's well-being.

The external world helps neither one nor the other. We are bombarded with baseless vulgarity, with a motley mass of messages and hollow trivia, with relentless slogans and quick fire changes that leave no time to be seen or appraised. Any information service (e.g., television) that we access in the hope of seeing something serious leaves us disappointed. Our scramble for solutions is often not just virtual, but actually creates the problems it seeks to address.

A context of this kind, cannot help a still developing child to construct an identity out of his/her natural inclinations and personal, actualizing potential, that is, to become a person who is able to deal with the complexity of the real world, and who knows how to use virtual reality without being at its mercy or confusing it with something else.

Since this kind of narcissism is a recent phenomenon, there is still a lack of clinical case records describing its functional and pathological consequences, as well as appropriate modes of treatment. At present, young people in this type of difficulty are cared for by social services, in children's psychiatric wards and by volunteers who by chance or circumstance find themselves looking after them.

Many thanks to Dr. Valeria Ugolini, psychologist and psychotherapist at Ferrara public health service (Department of Integrative Assistance, Mental Health and Psychological Addictions), for her help in writing these notes on virtual narcissism.

3 Psychotherapy and the process

"We are such stuff as dreams are made on"
William Shakespeare

The therapeutic process unfolds through several stages and, little by little, through the strata of one's personality (structure), moves from the surface down to deeper parts where original conflicts and unsolved problems lie. It can take some time before entering the flow of *"Being" of the present and the "having been" of the past.*

In order to make things simple and descriptive, explaining a work that has complex scientific and clinical rules, I have managed to "locate" certain steps (schematic diagrams) in the process. Psychotherapy is a flow of words- dreams- images- events past and present- memories and so on. A sort of **Jigsaw puzzle to be RE-ASSEMBLED.**

My Master Carl Rogers used to say *"... clients must be left free to "range freely" in their world. It is important to let them go wherever they need. They are the only ones who know the story, and their telling is like water springing from a source and, as it flows, it will find its way towards the sea... the ocean of life".*

If water flows free, it will form natural gorges, find and form its bed, its banks...so it will flow according to its nature, rhythm, capabilities. Sometimes in my explanations, I shall use the word "person", other times I shall use the personal "we", since we are all bearers of pages and pages of a story written in our "being".

"Along the way" I shall often summarize the steps. It helps keep hold of the "gestalt" in its whole.

When we START the "journey" of a psychotherapy, at the beginning, we move through a period of *"complaints"*. Complaining about things that are not going well. About a troubled life, abuse of power suffered from others, abuse caused to others. Failures in relationships, failures in the world, with ourselves. Talking about oneself in this guise is comprehensible, since at this stage, we can only "see" what goes wrong but unable to understand "why" this happens. This is the beginning, the surface of a "tortuous" journey… Often, in the first session the person brings up various problems, talks about malaise and bad luck occurring over and over again, complains and cries. It is the cry of one who is living expecting that someone in the world will satisfy those ancient needs. Alas, expectation is vain and bitterness keeps on growing. **These needs have become "strawberry ice cream".**

Why such a "fate?"…

Over the years, the person has built *a distorted structure of the Self* and, now moves in the world with dysfunctional patterns but is unaware of this. On the contrary, he has a rooted conviction that the trouble is coming from "outside"; hence a general dissatisfaction and resentment toward the world.

The therapeutic work and the unfolding process of the Self will consist of the elaboration of experiences, frustrations, sufferings, conflicts, fears and a search into the present and into the past of 'how" facts take place, "what" happens and "why" it happens.

In the FOLLOWING STEP, the focus is specifically on matters concerning others, family members, or acquaintances…Their behaviours are often perceived to be frustrating. Interactions are difficult. The cry: ***"Others"*** do not change …

The work, so far described, along with the feelings experienced by the client and their complaints, could be considered a waste of time. However, it is in the client's power to move as he feels, and it turns out to be crucial for starting a work of "introspection". It helps to discover how we play "our cards", how others, in turn, play "their" game. The client starts to ***realize, on a cognitive level,*** how these games (dynamics) interweave, giving rise to frequent misunderstandings.

At a deeper level, there is an unfolding of *dynamics, concerning "what happens"*, how it happens, and "WHY" it happens. Thanks to the **contact** with the emotions that surface and by connecting them with facts coming to light, thanks to emotions regarding our reactions toward others (I –Thou), emotions having to do with ourselves (I – Me),   we now understand the uneasiness we experience when interacting with others. We discover how and why some relationships are so unhappy and dissatisfying or deteriorated or even insane…

The client connects with the "REAL SELF". With the present story. With fragments of the past years. *PAST AND PRESENT superimpose alternately.*

The journey into the ego, leads to **places** of our past, which are deposits of feelings, of positive and negative contents. Negative because they are not accepted or are too hurtful to "handle". These "places" become the revival of our experiences when we were left in loneliness to cope with ourselves and with the world. Places where we have set aside painful experiences, too difficult to "hold" on to, too confused to deal with, too weak to react, and frightening because we are unable to face reality or "living in the world". We can find fragments of our story again, forgotten emotions. There is a return of emotions in the form of recollections or images. Often the client says "…I already knew that, but it was kind of buried somewhere in my mind…" We recognize the wounds, the voids, the dreams built with so much hard work. The craving for our needs. The fears that lie in the structure of the "Being"… for a lifetime … (especially in cases of abuse).

Travelling backwards and into the inner self, through processes in which the way of being is unsustainable, in which situations are obstructing personal power from coming out, we shall have to **relinquish** those *special structures* set up in the attempt to build relationships with the world and with others for the satisfaction of our needs and voids.

It is important to bear in mind that going back to the past or reading the present, are not sufficient to bring a change in our inner world. It is necessary to go through the elaboration of a **"mourning"**. We must build up the **knowledge** first, reach **consciousness** later, and then we must **relinquish** *"what was not given in the past", (It is a funeral).* We must give up "dreams" built upon the "not given". The therapist will respect the reconstruction of the vicissitudes, just as the client brings them up.

Sometimes, even though we realize that the behaviours adopted, are against our "freedom to be", even though we clearly see when we are victims or abusers, we are unable to change. Though causing us troubles, these behaviors are the *best and the* **maximum** *we can do. Situations are to be given the dignity of "being".*

As we have already seen, there are always "good reasons" why we persist in the same behaviour. These **very good reasons** are the ones to find, analyze and understand. If it is not possible to change them, they need respect, consideration, and to be accepted as "citizens of the world". The therapist must leave the client free to move, stay still, be confused, be angry, according to his/her rhythms. The structures we built during our early years are the outcome of great efforts, the **utmost** we were capable of achieving.

When we mention "a change " of our behaviour, it means **"dismantling"** those structures so painfully built, then, giving rise to *"ways of being in the world"* related to ourselves and to others. This takes place if we have patience and take all the time we need.

A CLIENT: **"...*I am still in need of long absences. Maybe our endeavour is a potent request of respect and legitimate silence...*"**

As soon as the defensive structure is discarded, our need/search for external support slows down and this means we have less need of someone else. All that energy used in vain to receive "strawberry ice creams" from the outer world is now there to achieve self-evaluation.

There is a firm consciousness of **one's own being,** no longer saturated with feelings and experiences of an unsolved past. The relation between oneself and things is straightforward and *"played"* in the **"here and now".** For example, if you deceive me, I get angry with you at once. There is no "waiting for another moment". It is very important not to invest the anger with meanings other than the deceit just suffered. There is no longer the "I am angry because this reminds me that, years ago, my father, my mother, blah, blah…".

4 Defensive structures and mourning

Harmful aspects of significant others

We mentioned the removal of defensive structures representing neurotic patterns used in relating with the world and ourselves. They are neurotic structures built to escape conflicts and sorrows of the past but that we keep on using in the present, in all our relationships, both positive and negative. As long as the neurotic mechanism is used, it happens that: **"if a part of our life has been damaged by others, the other part is being destroyed by us!"** We spend a great amount of energy and strength in the attempt to understand and change others with the hope of obtaining what we need, instead of making a change in ourselves. An oriental philosopher says, *"When we have succeeded in understanding ourselves, we will not need to understand others because we see them"*.

Only by *giving up our dreams*, going *through mourning and the healing of wounds,* can we understand the origin of our problems. We must "die to ourselves" in order to be re-born, re-turn to ourselves, to the real essence of what we are. If we do not accept the **impotence** of our inner child and accept that **we have lost the game**, we are doomed to anger and fear. Our painful wounds will keep on bleeding.

The mourning or "the battle", as it were, is between Past Reality and Present Reality.

Past Reality:

* Frustrations – Dream.

* Wounds

* Voids

Example:
Need: appreciation – nearness
Frustration: never satisfied
Dream: appreciation- nearness
Wound: mortification – aggressiveness -conflicts
Reality: will never happen
Void: never filled
Present Reality:
* Nobody can satisfy those needs.
* Impossible to change one's story
* Relinquish the dream
* Fill the void with void
* Heal the wounds
Another important aspect we must come to terms with is that our positive or negative relationships with other people might be "in congruency" with ourselves but not with the outside world. Harmony means being in **congruency** with my **inner Self** and the **"universe"**. We shall see this in the last chapter.

Besides having to give up our dreams, we then must change the "patterns" we had been using in the attempt to satisfy the craving.

Example: *I always smile to receive benevolence - I cry hoping to receive compassion - I become a doormat hoping that my abuser might spare me or fall in love with me - I am at your disposal for anything as long as you accept me into your world… and so on.*

Unfortunately, behaviours built with mechanisms of our neurosis do not yield the reactions expected, but yield the opposite and have no explanation: "why… What have I done ... Why am I treated like this?"… It is a sign of the failure and reiteration of old patterns.

We can deduce that the behavioural patterns adopted are our attempts to realize our dreams, thus satisfy our needs. There we are with our attitudes – styles we adopt in relating with others –our emotional drives, powerfully guided by the will to satisfy our needs and eventually realize our dreams. All this is but the premise of a failure since others do not respond according to what we were longing for.

Nevertheless, should our expectations be satisfied, our need will not disappear, but will appear again… and again in an endless mechanism until the neurotic core is dissolved. Why? Because even though I can find the way to be satisfied, (satisfy the primary need) there is still "The Wound" of the negative experience in our past...

The dream is the craving for what "you did not give me".

The wound is the bleeding for what "you did to me".

The journey into those inner parts that we must uncover in order to find the meanings of our behaviour, leads to coming into contact with the child we were: **our inner child**. The "little one", takes **shape** through behaviours and emotions experienced by the **adult part** that is "wounded" in the **present world**. Feelings and emotions that wind way back into the PAST.

Let us take an example of a client who finds her inner child and says "*...I am stunned. Judy is my best friend, but she treats me like a door mat... and I do become a door mat and pretend I am not hurt when she wrongs me, when she offends me, when she offers a piece of cake to everyone else except me. I pretend I am not hurt... and I smile...and... and shame flows into my bones... (silence)... also when I was little I behaved like that...(cries— silence)...I used to be unfairly blamed... also in front of other people... I was full of shame but I would smile... always* **afraid to be left alone**". Now she understands why, when ill treated she is incapable of reacting; nevertheless she still "curls up" in her inner world exactly as when she was a little girl.

Her Smile: It is channeled sorrow, a concealed shame. It is the stoned powerless pain... it is the unheard wound. When the client comes to these insights, her adult part has got the "past reality" into focus. However, the understanding does not lead to a change, since there is an incapacity to behave in a different manner. Now the client is "starting" to become aware of her behaviours and of "their good reasons". That **spotlights the hidden reasons.**

Another example:

Mary has no children. With great discretion she takes care of her sister's children, of their development, of how her sister and brother-in-law behave toward them. She gives a lot of presents, helps with their homework. In a session she complains: "*...Whatever I do, I see that the kids are detached... They are ungrateful...*". Later she understands that her "good reason" in doing all this was **her expectation**: a *mother and child* love **she is expecting** from these children. Realizes that the "way" she was taking care of them, was "what she, Mary" had been expecting from her own mother. "Mary" is the "little girl" who would have been so warm and grateful toward her mummy... Maybe Mary is indeed very kind– more caring than their parents, but her nephews and nieces will never react with the filial love she is expecting. She is regarded only as an auntie. The **filial love was "a dream"**. It took Mary a long time before giving up her need. When she succeeded in experiencing herself just as an auntie, the relationship improved.

The manners adopted in such relationships are our *dreams* transformed into *patterns that fail,* because "the other" does not respond to our expectations. The process for the elaboration of these conflicting aspects is long and complex. Games constantly repeated. Suffering is conscious, vivid and bitter. The price we pay is heavy. Fears and dreams that surface, in the attempt to "change the game", are now much clearer and **"dignity"** starts growing …But the games keep going on with the same old rules and patterns.

Thus, I repeat what I said above: Once you know how and why you play the game, the problems are not over…

Nevertheless, it is important to bear in mind that when we try to get out (rid) of consolidated dynamics (games) or interactions, the outside world ("others") is not willing to "welcome" the change we struggle to make. It is the contrary. Since there is a habit (a tacit consent!) to interact with the old pattern/behaviour, there could be resentful reactions and sometimes aggressiveness. These mechanisms are an attempt to hamper the change. Female murder is an example. Why so? Because the change in one of the partners, implicates a change also in he who interacts with that person. Sometimes there is no willingness to change adaptive strategies.

It is not simple to describe a process of change and growth. Phenomenology has no theories, because it is an "experiential" change. However, it is possible to point out some important aspects by spotlighting certain events and their origin.

I shall talk about:

Obstinacy: the mechanism we use in order to have *"dreams and needs become true".* I call the tools **silver threads or silver strings.** Friedrich Nietzsche says, *"We are made with the stuff of our dreams"* …

Strawberry ice cream: symbol of the dream. A specific need. It is **"running on empty…"**

Green apples: The "true" reality in family dynamics.

Red apples: The "idealized" reality that we struggle to build in place of "true reality/green apples".

Mourning: a process of "relinquishing". A hard, painful process in psychotherapy is to **dismantle** *structures and dreams* set up in the past to save us, to hide our sorrows. Now they have become an obstacle to the development of our "personal power", since they hinder the flow of our formative tendency.

Another important aspect to consider is how deep **we buried or denied our emotions.** When we bury them, they are there emitting their sounds, but when we deny them, they are "cast away" and become for us a "not me". It will take a long time to get them back and become part of our story. We shall see this later: experience denied or distorted.

The "way of being in sufferance"

Before moving into the main aspects concerning frustration and failing strategies, I shall begin from **where our problems originate.**

All I need

A child has the right/need to receive warmth and love. He/she has the right/need to receive unconditional care and positive regard from the "caregivers".

Warmth and love. "*I enfold you in a symphony of love*".
"*love does not need to forgive, because it does not feel injured*".

During the early years of life, interactions are mainly with members of the family. Family is the only basis of evolution and experience. It is also the basic unity of mental health or illness.

What might happen

It might happen that relationship with caregivers, the environment, circumstances of life, give evidence of something that is an obstacle to the development of the child's "organismic Self". **Such experiences hamper** "actualizing tendency" and development of the True Self. They are experiences *denied or distorted*. These aspects/experiences cause

Wounds and Voids

The child/WE are not able to cope with **such a reality,** differing from what we need. Sometimes it is marked by quarrels, harshness, cold-heartedness, ill-treatment, physical or psychological abuse, over-protection, carelessness, strictness, obsessiveness, inconsistent behaviours, excessive punishments, unpredictability and so on.

In this climate, the experiences and feelings of the growing child are mainly of not being loved, not noticed, not considered, not listened to, not accepted, not helped, valued only on certain conditions, incapable of understanding distorted messages.

The environment can be like a "hard world", disturbed by the dynamics working on incoherence and ambiguity. Equivocal messages, realities that are everything but also the opposite, lovingness conditioned by dominant child-raising dogmas, ill treatment, physical or sexual abuse.

In order to survive the child needs to *"draw a veil"* over the wounds caused by such painful experiences. Even though hidden, wounds will bleed…

"Wounds are what you did to me" – "Voids are what has not been"

In place of "what has not been", there appears a **"void"** and in the child's magical world, a *dream* **comes creeping in.** Such a dream will soon or later satisfy a need. **Wounds** are "what you did to me"; "why you hurt me"; "what have I done?"

Void and dreams… A strawberry ice cream and Silver threads

Here is the **"source"** of *behavioural patterns*/**strategies** that should allow the child to receive from caregivers, and later on, from the outer world, fulfillment of those needs, in other words, to make dreams come true. Unfortunately, they are patterns set up to cope with "troubled" relationships.

The tool used to "carry out this job" is a thread/**Silver Threads** wound around the person in order to receive the "precious nectar": the not given.

Red Apples against Green Apples

Later, when the child reaches adulthood, he/she builds an idea of how to set up a family that should be exactly the opposite *(red apples)* to what was experienced *(green apples)*.

All through life, the struggle will be to achieve those dreams. This is the **reason for all our troubles.**

We shall move into the world with our "silver strings" through which we are "sure" to receive the "nectar" we have been longing for. **THE CRAVING…**

Some of us try to do away with wounds and voids by using another "method": **Denial.**

If we deny all feelings and emotions caused by the wounds, **we** are destined to **repeat** patterns of the bitter reality we went through. It is a strong defence mechanism, but harmful for ourselves since our feelings and emotions have been rejected, silenced, but also painful for partners and our children. These are dynamics where **the role of victim and abuser are confused.**

Where is the "trap"? Where is the "blind" side of our "being"? **If these ways of being are a failure, what is the right pathway? Where is Reality?**

Using a metaphor, we could say that we should look and live with our **"poisoned"** apples: *our reality.* This would save us from poisoning our existence when adults…whereas, we dream of the "red apples" because in the past **there was nobody there** to help us "stay" in the "here and now". Nobody to help me *contain* my feelings, to *understand* what's going on.

Given its age, a child is in a situation marked by impotence, sense of limits, incapability of doing something, of understanding. As a result, fear, a sense of loneliness and sometimes a paralyzing terror, become part of our experience. **What is missing? "Containment" by an adult figure.**

In adulthood, when we are in need of help, the **"containment"** lacking in childhood will be provided by the psychotherapist. Once a client said *"I see you like this: a therapist who takes you by the hand when you are about to fall, and* **helps you BACK onto the thread** *into the precarious balance of life"*.

It is important to point out that in **the case of** defensive mechanisms set up in order to **DENY one's story**, (the "not me defence" H.S.Sullivan) personality structures are built with interchanging sadistic and victimizing models, as described above. It is a complex personality. The problem is explored in the last chapter.

It often happens that a caregiver, a relative, a friend, a dictatorial person can, by mistake, **put pressure** on a child in order to shape his/her behaviour and life, according to certain patterns and principles. The therapeutic process helps to **take back possession** of a *"freedom to be"*, to get rid of the influence from the physical or psychological presence of the other person. The hard core consists in having to give up many needs and dreams. It is a **"price to pay"**…

5 The story of the self

How it should have been

If parents were respectful of one's personality, that is, taking the inexperienced "human puppy" by the hand during the development of the Self, **WE,** the puppy, would not start craving for the "red apple" or the "strawberry ice cream" since it would exist, integrated in the "being" of the here and now. Once grown up, we will not need them since we "ate" them (experienced) in childhood "from the right source".

Experiencing one's potentialities to the full, in an accepting atmosphere, is the key to growing up toward **freedom in respect of oneself and others.** Acquiring a **Personal Power** is the maximum expression of the **actualizing tendency,** (Rogers).

The actualizing tendency is our organism's tendency to develop capacities necessary for maintenance and validation of the organism. It is a development toward autonomy, away from the control of the outer-world. "Elan vital" is an energy drive towards life. Its hindrance causes destructive reactions for our organism.

(…) An adult asked the Master "talk to me about my sorrows". The Master answered: "When children are growing, they need unconditional love and positive regard. To grow being listened to. To be seen, considered, appreciated and facilitated in their doings…"

Children have nothing to give in return, when young. They will give back love later, "beyond" having or not having received love. They "need to be loved". Should a child have antisocial behaviour, as some parents complain, it is a signal that something distorted is already underway. Something happened in the outside world and it is never the child's fault.

A "betrayed" love will hamper autonomous growth and tie the child in a relationship of dependency with the caregiver, early on and later with the outer world. It may be conformism, rebellion, or other behaviours.

It is important to bear in mind that when considered a "difficult" boy or a "difficult" girl or a "rebellious" character, the child is actually a **wounded creature** and highly dependent on the caregiver. It is important to distinguish a biological dependency from a neurotic dependency. The first is positive because it allows the child to bring nourishment to his "being a Person". It fosters a natural detachment from the family and confidence in **going into the world**. In the second case, child and caregiver are unable to "untie" each other.

The child is "trapped" in the adult's problems from the past.

What is the way out?

What is the way to get out of our troubles? By going back to our life story. The only way out is the **"reality of what has been"**.

To synthesize we live with **four realities**.

* In the "background" there is *"what should have been"*.

* Another level is the reality of *"what really happened"*.

* Third comes the *"reality we Dream"*.

* Last but not least: *"The Present Reality"* influenced by the other three.

***The only way out is **"to go through"**.

Here are some specific aspects:

Silver strings

Let us consider the needs we incessantly try to satisfy. We can imagine them like "silver strings". We carry them with us "wherever we roam". We try to wind them around others (or situations) in an attempt to have our needs satisfied. It is also a way we use to be tied to the other person (dependency). The string is the metaphorical description of the dreams and needs we try at all costs to satisfy. Sometimes it is mainly for this that we live…

The strings around the other person are searching for the nourishment denied in childhood. It is a nourishment that will never satisfy our "inner child". The strings will prove to be "useless".

So, why all this hard work in pursuing a kind of vicious circle without solution? If the fountain (Caregiver) was dry and never gave the water we demanded, we go around the world, searching for "that" kind of fountain and "that" water. It must be that one and no other. Alas, fountains of that type will never give "that" water. Should we meet other springs of cool water we will not notice them. We do not like them. We may be gratified, but we will never fall in love with that spring. We may happen to find the right fountain, but the water given will never be enough.

WHY?… Because "a caregiver or significant other" is UNIQUE.

This explains the worldwide complaint: "why do I keep on meeting people who make me suffer? It is the consequence of wanting to experience our lives through our silver strings, in the illusory hope that someone else, soon or later, shall satisfy our needs or fulfill our desires.

How can we end the game with our past? *By healing the wounds* of our sorrows and voids. We must relinquish our dreams by ***"filling the void with void"… and heal the bleeding wounds by accepting reality.***

Strawberry ice cream

Strawberry ice cream is a metaphor. Metaphors, commonly used in psychotherapy, trigger imagination. The advantage is to reach the fields of emotions and feelings bypassing rational process.

Strawberry ice cream represents a specific but unsatisfied need in our story. In childhood, there are needs to be satisfied, in order to build our identity, our self-esteem and so on. We need "that" colour and "that" taste, from "that" specific person, and in "that" specific period or moment. The "not given" sets up interactions/silver strings with others with the aim of filling that void.

They are specific requests, specific like the requests made to "that" specific person (Significant other). It is an illusion since the need made sense originally and **only** from our caregivers.

Sometimes, beside the void, there can be wounds caused by the need: "I need to be accepted just as I am". It can happen that, besides not being satisfied (respected) in my need, I am "punished" because I am not as you want me to be. This opens a "bleeding wound". Thus, strawberry ice cream represents a "void" and a "wound".

In adulthood we shall always attempt to attain the "not given" by putting certain patterns into practice that will turn out to be a failure. This causes frustration, further voids and more wounds. They are the "silver threads" created with a great consumption of energy, but that we wind around others and to which we desperately cling in the attempt to satisfy our craving.

In a session a client said: **"dreams serve to cover void and wounds"**

The following is Nancy's dream.

For many years, Nancy pursued the dream to receive consideration and appreciation from her father for "her way of being" and not only for how she, so obedient, behaved to please her father's needs. She accepted rigid moral values In order to obtain what "she" needed: to be seen for how "she" was. As years went by, she realized that those values did not correspond to her "true" way of being, and moreover that no one would ever "see her". Her father, closed in a world of his own, was interested only in having his family share his same values, and behave accordingly. There was no way he would ever leave room for any other vision of the world.

There was no space for him to accept Nancy's true nature. She was not aware of this. She would adapt to everything… *"in order to be seen".*

Now she is an adult and adapts to all her boyfriend's moods waiting to "be seen", to be recognized and share her needs and desires. Even though she accepts all his demands and bouts of bad temper, the young man has no attention for her, but he even blames her: *"…you should have understood, even if I didn't say anything".*

Nancy went through a process of elaborating guilt toward her father, her boyfriend, and even toward herself: *"I haven't even the right to say to myself that I suffer for my father's offenses",* for the values imposed upon her, but not shared by her. At a certain point, she encountered feelings and needs so different from her father's, and experienced feelings of freedom. Nevertheless, the idea of relinquishing those strict rules that *"gave me self-confidence",* made her feel all the pain of bidding farewell to the *"difficult but safe companions of my life".* (Since the "organismic Self" could not give her any landmarks, those rigid values made her feel safe). In that period, along with this relinquishing, also the *dream of her life* "to be seen", was fading away.

It was important to "walk" very slowly with Nancy in her

exploration. Besides the mourning of a dream, she had to "make her way" out of patterns that were not hers. Now and then she was overwhelmed with fear: *"…and afterwards? …Patterns have been my security… what shall I do afterwards?… What can I do? …How can I know? …These schemes have never been mine. Which are mine?"…* Only going through layers of pain and gaining consciousness of her "experiencing" (no one can tell her what to do) Nancy changed her feelings and behaviours, thus gaining self-esteem and Personal Power.

How can this come about?

The first stage consists of experiencing deeply what is going on. It is ***cognitive knowledge,*** in touch with the emotional inner world. Sometimes, before this, the client goes through a period when the "here and now" is experienced only on a "cognitive level". If the therapist asks, "what are you feeling", the answer is "I am thinking that…". This is an understanding/perceiving one's behaviours "mentally", having lost contact with the emotional world.

Later, there is a shift towards *"feeling what is happening to me".* At this stage, there is ***consciousness*** of deep uneasiness. At a certain point, it becomes unbearable and we react against so much suffering. (I say that the ***"grass of dignity is starting to grow"***…). Courage comes deep from the "guts" and the "consciousness" of what is going on: a ***flash of respect*** for oneself. It is a moment when one says: "That's enough". **Dignity and worth** are like flowers springing up from the bottom of wounds caused by all the wrongs suffered. Self-respect, love and transparency are values that save our Personal Power and Dignity.

In other situations, the mainspring for change comes from the decision to "accept" the situation/reality for what it is, at that moment of life. My experience as a psychotherapist provides evidence that this counts also for child victims of all kinds of abuse. Salvation goes through the recognition of "being defeated"; losing the game.

Working with children, the first stage of the process is mediated through a story integrated with the child's experience:

An example:

The abused child was playing with a sword and shouting:

Child: "I am a strong prince! I can destroy my enemies!"

Therapist: …a prince might lose a battle…
Child: Nooo!
Therapist: …*That does not mean the prince weak and he is no longer a hero.* This means recognizing defeat and being in a condition of "impotence" (Very difficult for a child to accept.)
Child: …I shall think about this!.
I shall not go further into this aspect but just point out that, in order to be able to "re-emerge" from one's wounds, it is necessary to **"sink" into the sea of sorrows and fears** of **reality,** of how things occurred.

The Dream

A dream is a frame set up with the aid of tools typical in childhood: a magic idea – powerful thought – creativity – principle of pleasure. The dream replaces the void caused by what is "not satisfied".

A dream is the illusion, the promise the young child sets up to satisfy the need. "I will succeed… be given what I need… soon or later I will succeed"… and walks in the stream of life with his silver threads…

Later it will be the adult, who will go roaming with the inner-child, searching/craving for the same need. When failures show up, they will never say, the child first and then the adult that failures are due to the dreams that cannot work since they will never satisfy needs. Failure turns out to be "their" fault: "it is I who can't find the right way", and this goes and joins with the feelings of frustration, of shame, of mortification, of low esteem towards oneself and of rage toward the other.

The Void

The void pertains to the needs and later to the dreams that are never satisfied. … Alas… In their place there should be reality. REALITY is waiting…*The unpleasant part of our story. The actual reality. The reality experienced.*

It is necessary to mourn the loss of the dream. This means giving up the need and accepting the true reality. On the contrary, in our daily life, we reiterate patterns set up in the attempt to satisfy the need. Patterns fed by our dreams and by an unending search and craving.

The red apples

Sometimes the reality we experience is bitter. A reality having to do with *family dynamics, and a painful atmosphere*. I call it "green apples". When it is too difficult to cope with, we set it aside with all its emotions and fears, and **replace it** with a desire corresponding to what we would like to have. This is the reality of the "red apples", so we devise behaviours that "should be able" to satisfy the need.

An example:

June is seeking situations allowing her to "stay in peace". She chooses behaviours/strategies with the aim of obtaining what she desires and getting away from the hell she is living in at home.

June comes from a family that was "a complete ruin". *"I was scared, paralyzed, wouldn't even breath. My father would shout and throw whatever he found".* June tried to save herself from a sort of destruction and from being lost in such degradation, by learning how to react and manage to keep everything from crumbling.

When she met Martin, a man without a job and *"in bits and pieces"*, she said it was easy for her to handle and cope with all the troubles (green apples) and *"settle everything down"* in order to create the "once dreamed of" atmosphere, the taste of "red apples". The long craved "sweet nectar of home".

What did she do? With Martin, she behaved exactly like when she was at home: found a job, started working and maintained him for every need, but Martin had a bad temper, was always unsatisfied and would become destructive… just as in her family.

Another example: pieces from a session.

Mirko was talking about his family with "double bind communication" dynamics. A mother unable to be caring. A compulsive and raging father. I gave him feedback using a metaphor as follows: "amidst a world of garbage, I see a child in a market place searching amongst the waste. *"Pieces of something he could eat"*… Mirko answers. *"It reminds me of when I was a child and my dad would ask me to do something, I pretended to do it with utmost care, meticulously, so it would take me a long time. I never wanted to finish because I knew I had to face his critical, devastating remarks and often his whacks. Most of the times I couldn't understand why… there were no reasons for doing so".*

Sometimes, when the rages burst out, everything was out of control. Inability to do anything would creep up on Mirko. Fear welled up, with the feeling of no protective arms around him. Moreover, his mother would make him feel guilty and confused because instead of protecting her son in some way, she would force the child to go to his father and say: "I forgive you for what happened". Scared but wanting to get out of such a situation as soon as possible, the "innocent child" would obey, but would then manage to get himself involved in doing something in a meticulous and obsessive manner. This made him concentrate hard so he could forget what happened, control his feelings and his "confusion" about reality: "Where is the truth? Who is right? Who is wrong"?

Obsession became a prison to his Self.

The voids and wounds I buried
The pains and sorrows I forgot
The silver threads I enveloped
have become my prison
They lie in silence
within the folds of my soul
But when reality shows up
their cords quiver
The void that along
the road of my life
was hollowed out
sends plaintive vibrations
But that I immediately
BURY

Now Mirko is an adult. When he is about to leave his office at the end of the day, a turmoil of thoughts and fears fills his mind. His terror is that during his absence, something "terrible" might occur. He has the feeling he's leaving things at the "mercy" (his words) of the unknown, of negative events, and he would be helpless and guilty. The "pieces" of his childhood experience that he was unable to cope with, and had to hide deep inside his "silenced" wounds, have found a way to make themselves heard: they have ended up in his **present "irrational" fears**. *The "real" fears of the past are still calling...*

Along the pathway of psychotherapy, he realizes that when there are important festivities, he gathers his family with the "hope" (dream) of producing the "red apples" of a "crib family". This is how he figures it.

He wants to turn his "family in ruins" into "heavenly peace". He engages in a number of preparations for the event. When it's all over there is always a feeling of sadness, because things did not turn out according to his expectations. Even though he tried with all his strength to create a comfortable atmosphere, the "actors" were always the same as when he was a child…

Daniela.

A well-known pediatrician unable to enjoy her successful profession. When babies' parents thank her for the skill and success in dealing with the little patients, a bitter cry wrings her heart. The cry belongs to that little girl (her inner child) who knows how hard and painful the road of the "obedient child" has been, in the vain attempt to be seen and acknowledged by her parents. In other words, the present joy and praise awaken the hidden pain, wounds and void. We can say "love is my enemy". What happens? The cords of lovingness and recognition (*love*) coming from her clients, stimulate the cords of pain and sorrow *(sad memories)*.

Sara.

For a few weeks, Sara has been experiencing feelings of "precariousness" as regards herself, in contrast with a perception of "appreciation" coming from others. She has doubts about her professional capabilities. Her colleagues are much better. Her career is threatened. During an interview it turned out that the feeling of incapability she was experiencing was actually a feeling pertaining to her "inner world".

From a clinical point of view, this is a "shift" from an outside to an inside reality. ***An uneasiness*** ascribed to the "outside world", in order to ***escape*** from a pain springing up in her "inner world". "Unfinished business" as George De Rita would say! As we can see, the "outside" perception was the "symbolic representation" of her inner world. Even though concealed, it was sending its cries.

"Contact" made with the inner parts puzzled Sara. All the structures built to cover the remote parts of her painful story are shaking. It's the story of a little girl, who collected many failures with the hope of **receiving esteem and acceptance** just as she was, with "her" talents and "her" temperament according to her actualizing tendency.

During a session she says: *"…Once I put "Jif" (a cleaning agent) on the taps in the bathroom and mum got into a bad temper and scolded me. I went to her saying "Sorry mummy. Forgive me". I knew I was false because I wanted something else… I wanted her to behave in a different manner… to say to me "don't worry my dear, it doesn't matter". I wanted and now still want to be part of her world and not kept out like a stranger (weeping)… She only says do this do that … but me… I wanted something else from her…she is an iceberg".* Here she stops and says: *"I don't want to go any further, because now, all this is "behind". It is what I have been building…".* She does not want to go deeper into her story of life. I respected her request.

Today Sara "needs/is craving" for success and approval: *"Should I fail, I feel that for me it's the end".*

If approval does not arrive, she feels rejected and excluded. Just the way she felt excluded from her mother's world, in spite of all the strength she had been investing, meeting all her mother's requests with the attempt to be accepted, to "be seen".

The strategies adopted to have a "human touch" with her mother caused the child Sara so much pain, wounds and voids, that now the adult shrinks from any possibility of failure. Unbearable. She would feel devastated. As regards her relationship with her boyfriend, she told him she wants to get "inside" him. To be in his world, to enjoy being "in human touch". Her "strawberry ice cream!"

Relinquishing dreams (Coming to terms with reality)

How can we heal the wounds of our sorrows? We must give up the dream by accepting the **truth/reality** of our story. Dreams must turn back into reality. Right! How can one afford to relinquish the dream? The adult part, who has developed a "critical view/sense of reality" must recognize that the "not given" in childhood will never be given by the caregivers, or by anyone else. Nobody, from the outside world, can fill that void. The nurturing needs of childhood were important during the developmental stage. The "hard work" consists of accepting the "reality" of the **NOT GIVEN /VOID** and exploring the **WOUNDS** caused by our caregivers and hidden in the "darkness" of our inner world. Listen to the pain and fears. Look into pieces of our story set aside and face those hidden pieces of our "puzzle" of life.

The "sacred" strawberry ice cream the child had all the rights to "eat at the fountain of love" will never arrive. If we do not give it up, when we eat a chocolate ice cream, our inner child will say: "yes… it's nice…but that strawberry ice cream…" Chocolate ice cream is not appreciated in itself, because it is spoilt by the sadness for the "not given". We can try to fill the void/not given with something else (a surrogate), but it will never be sufficient to fill the gap and the void will cry out its anger. Typical of angry and grumbling people, never happy. It is a bottomless pit and when the surrogate stops coming, the void gets *very angry.*

If we manage to let go of the desire forever, and this means "giving up" the craving, our chocolate ice cream is without the "bitter taste" of the ungiven. This is the only way out, because **the void fills only with its void.**

The pain I have forgotten
in my heart is burning,
in the dark
shores of my dreams.
The pain that hath forgotten its story
hath no words, but long sighs.
In the midnight darkness
there is no chant of birds
but chirping of crickets.
From: Sfulingo – Rabindranath Tagore.

My prayer to caregivers

An endless request to satisfy primary needs is manifest in the "annoying and wearisome" crying of children. The caregiver makes all kinds of attempts to "silence" the creature. It is in vain, because the child is asking for something the adult is unable or does not want to give.

Please answer their prayer… Listen to their needs and NOT yours.

And, The Master said:

*"Now you have grown up, but are still in need and searching what you were asking for. You still have a strong desire that others and also your parents should **admit** incongruousness and contradictions, because you need to know the truth. Nobody will ever tell you the truth; everyone has their own truth. These people too, are playing "the life-game of cards". Only your adult part, now reconciled with the world and healed by the truth:* ***they hurt me and no one can change*

what has been", will give you what you need and take care of your inner child. It is important that you believe in what you see and think. Only life can and will tell you if you are right or wrong. Remember that no one will give you the peace you are seeking. It will not be others, who can grant you confidence. You will find it within yourself and through your actualizing tendency. Confidence does not grow out of assurance given by others, but from your own trust and from your inner resources. When we ask the outside world for assurance, it is because we need to be sure that what we are going to do is right. In life, we can also make mistakes! It is important to be able to "take the risk" without the certainty of succeeding. This means trusting in oneself, in life, and in others.

The **void caused by the "not given" can be filled only with the void which "is" the experience of the not given.** It is part of your story. Once integrated as a part of the Self, thou shall cry no more. The problem is that you try at all costs to fill the void with surrogates or substitutes. The void will be a bottomless pit for whatever you put in it. It will always be empty. Feelings of failure, displeasure, empty struggles, mortification will come to an end when the need for **"dignity"** seeps into your consciousness. The process of giving burial to our dreams is starting and along with it, you start accepting **"limits** that are also the limits of life. Limits become part of the Self, when you decide to cut the silver threads".

Longing for lovingness
Lovingness
Lingers under the wounds
Caused by defeated losers.
As soon as Beauty
And Nature
And Smiles
open to my eyes
lovingness utters its painful cry and joy
and flings its hungry grasping arms…
But now… I know…
that Reality can come
and turn it into danger.

Healing wounds and filling voids

Conflicts caused by "careless hands" or distorted interactions within the family, will always be there. Neurotic patterns are rooted in the sorrow due to wounds caused by voids and frustrations, but all neurotic ways of being are a failure. We are no longer in touch with our actualizing tendency. It is our "distorted" Self, protected by "defensive mechanisms", that helps us to get away from "reality", a reality too difficult, too scary, or too painful to face, or to deal with. There is "incongruence" between *true feelings* and our way of being.

During the therapeutic process, we analyze our behaviours along with feelings of uneasiness, painful conflicts, and recollection of the past. We become aware of the reasons why we are swimming in "troubled waters"! We come to understand **when and why** we channeled our unbearable and painful reality into behaviours that are now causing so much trouble. We also figure out the patterns /strategies adopted in order to obtain what we are craving for and find out that they also are a failure. Voids caused by the "not-given", are always there. When we realize what we are doing, we get in touch with a **bitter feeling** owing to "empty" expectations and "painful experiences" for what has really happened. There is only "one way-out" and it consists of **"filling void with void and healings the wounds of reality"**.

It is impossible to explain how the story of life is unraveled. What happens is that little by little we gain consciousness of what happens, of frustrating experiences of the *past and present*. Facts, events, conflicts are uncovered by recognizing frustrations suffered in the present and past.

The **work** on *emotions and feelings* will heal the wounds by giving them acknowledgement and **"accepting that reality". New feelings of trust and self- confidence will surface.**

Behaviour will now be congruent and transparent in alliance with our actualizing tendency. The more we connect with the true Self, the higher is our awareness that the dreams and behaviours adopted to soothe our hungry hearts are failures. Just empty dreams. We recognize wounded parts of the self, still bleeding, and we must come to terms with the reality that caused them.

All this comes about through *awareness, acceptance and mourning:*

* What we have been craving will never be satisfied.

* The defensive mechanisms set up to cover bleeding wounds caused by caregivers and the environment, protected us but also worked against us.

* The "red apples" must turn back to "green apples" (reality).

* Silver threads/dreams must be cut down in order to "get hold"

of our Personal Power and be aware of our autonomous Self.

It is a steady work involving present and past reality. The more we understand the present with its emotions and behaviours and link it to our past, the more we reach the **nucleus** of our early sorrow, the **true pain of our existence.** The true pain that caused suffering we failed to face or cope with. It is **authentic sorrow,** in opposition to neurotic sorrow, which moves along an endless sterile pathway. This means there is a **"neurotic" sorrow** leading nowhere and a **"sorrow of Reality"** that ends.

We must **"die"** (a feeling) before this primary pain and sometimes cross the sea of submerged fear that nevertheless always sent plaintive sounds.

From the ashes of our dying, though painful, a feeling of loneliness and absolute loss along with a feeling of **"there is nothing else to lose"**, there arises a new feeling. A move towards a **BEING IN THE HERE AND NOW**, no longer linked to the past and no longer looking ahead (expecting), but in the **"NOW"** with SELF-DETERMINATION.

Psychotherapy is a process that "gives back" to children (to our inner child) **the "authentic" story.** It consists of putting in the right place the pieces (feelings and emotions that hold the truth) which at that time were too hard, too scary, or confusing, or unreadable to handle. The adult part with the aid of a therapist sees and reads reality. Reads it, in a clear version, both past and present, accepting it exactly as it is. **No longer striving to change others, but ourselves.**

From a poem:
OH Mother
Those moments when
we came across the same reality
you would ask me to hinder it.
And I ready and craving for love
would side with you
because, "yes, this time you saw me!"
We now would be together…at last!
I had won that place within you.
But later when I'd ask you:

"do you remember that time?...
remember that thing?...
remember how it turned out?"
You would answer:
"But... what thing?... when?...
You are raving"...
And once again I discovered that
you were not there .
(From: A psychotherapy? No... A lifetime.)

From a client

"I am facing life hand in hand with a child. I am well aware of the meanders of his heart. The enthusiasm of his hopes, the bitterness of his defeats, the wounds bleeding from humiliations. That child hides away, seeking protection in the solitary darkness; cold, black and silent like a night in a forest covered with snow. But... now and then he cannot resist: craving for light and warmth, he lights a small fire, a small flame of hope and for a short fatal instant, the flickering light becomes visible with his defenceless need for love he would like to receive. A short fatal instant to find himself once more defeated, humiliated. Thus in despair, he kills the fire with the icy snow and curls up once more in the dark, heavy obscurity. His desire is to die and if he does not die, it is because he knows, deep in his soul, that one night he shall light another fire. Maybe this time, to receive a caress on his cold little head. I sadly look at the little boy holding my hand tight. Maybe soon or later I shall stop whomever from approaching him. I shall hide him into my arms, no longer with the hope for that caress. No longer that small fire alight, I shall carry him in the world. A little desperate child".

From a letter

"...Today for the first time, still a little bit uneasy, I allowed myself some praise...I am sure I am clever, free... how can I say?... unique, "Personal"... I am feeling well... not a wonder-woman, but fully and serenely myself...I am feeling within me a feeling of pride never experienced before. The struggle to keep on improving, or better still, to be myself, continues. Though tough, it is enriching. A nourishment for the Self. Today I have found my treasure: Myself. I feel a great strength... and other beautiful things. The sensation is unique. I know you can understand. I want to let you know all this immediately. I do not want to wait fifteen days to share this with you". (She was in Rome for a conference).

The "adult part" of the Self realized, through the therapeutic process, that the strawberry ice cream is just a dream. One must let it melt away forever into "nothingness". The dream that sprang from a "void", from "nothing", goes back into "nothing".

Then there are the wounds for "what has been: harm suffered by distorted interactions. We must accept that things have gone "that way". Even though it was not our fault, nobody can change what happened. We must accept reality for what it has been.

The adult part, which had been depending on "other" than oneself, fades away. For some time, in us, a **veil of melancholy** will dwell owing to the clear understanding of how things really occurred.

The silver threads of which
I left slipping away from my hand
and with my dreams are flying away
far away.
Together with herons
they become small dots far away
and
they shan't be here
at the return of the herons
because that flight
is a going without return
and now I am free
From A psychotherapy?... no… a lifetime

The Master says:

"…You shall always be a child to whom it "was not given". You are one of many children who must say: "Not to me". Anyhow, rescued by your beautiful adult part. At the end of this long "voyage into the Self and inner world", the pieces of the puzzle you had lost or neglected, are now in their right place. No piece is missing and the witchery is that you are capable of recognizing the hidden or missing pieces.

*The cost is that you must come to terms with your **"impotence"** and that you **"have lost the game".***

You can now see your careless caregivers in their weakness and have warm feelings toward them. You shall no longer need to "understand" or judge the other, because you can see him/her. How did this happen? Because you have accepted reality as it was. You don't even need to forgive "your enemies" because "that is how things went." "That's it."

A Poem

Oh mother I looked at you
and there I found myself.
Before me was standing
my once sick little child
She was there outside of me
but now in the right place
A place that is within you.
I saw you frail and not loved
I recognized you and
at once loved you.
I shall never abandon you
and love you with that love
you have never known
how to give to me.
I am free…

Now, let us summarize a few concepts:

Void

The void originates in an **unsatisfied need.** We strive to fill our voids in order to escape from the "cry/pain" of the **"not given".** We use substitutes such as people, things, situations, patterns.

Sometimes we succeed in obtaining "the needed", but it is never enough. It is a bottomless pit. Even though we get what we want, there is an endless dissatisfaction.

Why? The void keeps uttering its painful cry since it is *unable to recognize the "filling".* Why? Because the "present" is not the story of our "past life". Those "cells" recognize and feed on what they need, only "at that time": each fruit has its own season.

Only our adult part will be able to fill the void and only by recognizing the story of the "Void". The Void itself is an experience of life and it is this experience that can "fill the void". **Void fills with void.**

"Illusions are but a clumsy attempt to fill the voids".

Wounds

Wounds originate in our early years of life. Destructive interactions with our caregivers. Frustrating and hurtful experiences within the family environment and from the outside world. Wounds keep on bleeding because we consider ourselves, and it is downright true, victims of lack of respect, unlovingness, little or no attention, and mortifications. Feelings and emotions, frustrations and resentment keep waiting for justice, but justice will never come. We must accept reality just as it is. Things went that way and nobody can change the painful story. As long as we keep on seeking recognition, we shall always bring along a feeling of frustration, sadness, depression, anger, but the dynamics with those people and situations will never change. We must give up hoping for changes and recognize we have **LOST THE GAME. Accept reality as it is.**

While we are doing all this work, feelings and emotions keep on changing: from anger or depression to fear and pain and anguish. Then comes self- esteem along with compassion and respect and lovingness for oneself and others. Trust in the True Self. At this point, in the last step, we work on a change in our behavioural patterns, and our frustrations turn into compassion towards our "enemies". **AND WE WILL LOVE OUR STORY.**

Integration

The first work of integration consists of "taking in and accepting," that is, giving acknowledgement to those "pieces of the broken mirror," we rejected and hid in the darkness and depths of our body, refusing to accept them as part of us. All our experiences must have the dignity to exist and be part of us and of our story. When the work is well done, we can really thank our enemies and love our story. IT IS COSMIC LOVE FOR OURSELVES.

To summarize, we reach **Integration of the Self** once we single out the **"inner child"** and the **"Patterns"** set up during early phases of life. We find aspects of "Being" that are defensive mechanisms and we understand that it turns out to be inadequate, a failure.

Sometimes it takes a long time to reach certain steps in the therapeutic process. Clients first talk about their troubles. Some do not know anything about underlying conflicts. The therapist can only help the client to cast light on what is going on and try to get hold of some sort of self- consciousness. It is a work of patience and respect toward whatever the client brings out. Rogers says: *"Stay with your client where ever he is, whatever he says, in congruency with his feelings and his frame of reference. His "river of life" in this free and respected flowing will lead him to the* **"ocean of life".**

The Master said:

…You will take over the task of protecting your "inner child", once set aside, after having accepted those parts you did not like; others you relinquished. After having found the "good reasons" why you distorted your Self, after acknowledging all these parts, after having changed the old obsolete pattern, after having come to terms with dreams and realities, after mourning for all you must change or leave behind, after accepting that you have lost the game, after having changed and discovered NEW FEELINGS AND EMOTIONS, this time WELLING UP from your FREE and CONGRUENT SELF, after this long process of mourning and integration, you will be able to **take your child hand in hand. Your inner child brings the gift** *of "Being without time". Its creativity. "Being in the Here and Now". The gift of being timeless enables you to enter the rhythm of life. You will look into the world with* **"eyes of wisdom".** *You will move along the pathway of life with the consciousness of* **"the Limits of things" and later, the "limits of being"** *(*we shall see this aspect further on).

When we change *from feelings and emotions belonging to our neurotic patterns* **and open on to** *the dawn of feelings pertaining to "Reality", an experience of sadness comes creeping up for how your life-story has been. Sadness has always been hiding between the lines of our story. In the long run, it will fade away and we will enjoy* **THE FREEDOM OF BEING.**

I shall leave you with the fragment of a poem:
emotions are rolling along
a hard bedded river.
"Have never heard you
silent and infinite presence
of my life".
"At last you heard me"
"Your name is melancholy, isn't it?"
"Yes. It's a long time I have been waiting…
A lifetime…
"Your face I recognized
but I never did like it"
"For years I've been here
For years I've been lonely.
I do not hear, I do not see
But your presence I feel

Take me, heal me, cuddle me....
The poem marks the beginning of Angelina's therapy.
From: A psychotherapy?..No… A lifetime

Letting go

It consists of reaching deep down to the core, where defensive mechanisms protected the little child from the realities and emotions too painful or difficult to handle.

This is the stage where we once again experience what remains: **the true reality**. Accept it for how it really was and how it is. We go again through those reactions, those feelings that were the only ones the child was able to deal with. The ones we carried along also in adulthood.

This is the moment when **we look back** and feel all the sorrow for the way things went. It is here where we lay down the strawberry ice cream forever, because this is its right place. "Letting go" is an experience that occurs only on condition that we "accept" **we have lost the game.**

When we reach this stage, the pain for the "not given", the pain for what actually happened, the pain and resentment at being hurt, are now healed. There is pleasure coming from so much work: **we did all this by ourselves.**

6 Considerations on wounds and destructive personalities

Violence and relationship

If our experience is destroyed
our behaviour will be destructive.
If our experience is destroyed
we have lost our own selves.

R.D. Laing

I only have a little experience with destructive personalities. Nevertheless I shall share the main aspects observed in my work.

Neuroscience could help us to work out the distortion of these experiences.

"…if you victim want to keep your relationship functioning, you must keep on doing what your partner wants. It has always been like that. The difference is that in the beginning, it was not noticeable since you anticipated your abuser in being at his/her disposal".

There are wounds inflicted by dysfunctional interactions between us and our caregivers, family members, environment, significant others, conflicts, violence in the early stage of our lives and later on in the outside world.

I would like to give an amusing touch to this sometimes "very painful" aspect with the aid of a biologist. I was at the Delhi airport with my dearest friend Somnath. He is professor of biology at the University of Delhi. At a duty free bookshop on the way to our gate, he bought me a book: "The Gene" by the famous gene biologist

Siddhartha Mukherjee. I thought he bought it because the day before we had a long talk about Autism. Once we reached our seats, I opened it. The Prologue was on the author's family. I read the first lines, burst out laughing and handed the book over to Somnath, but he was already laughing because he knew what it was about. The young man sitting beside me was watching the scene so I handed him the book. He read the few lines and now the three of us were laughing our heads off. The author was giving an ironic touch to a history of life, painful and traumatic. This is what we were reading:

They fuck you up, your mum and dad.
They may not mean to, but they do.
They fill you with the faults they had
And add some extra, just for you.
Philip Larkin, "This be the Verse"

Without doubt, Siddhartha is a person with a strong, cheerful temperament. This tells us something about "temperament" which is genetically determined, whereas our "character" is the result of our life history.

That is one of the reasons why brothers and sisters differ in the dynamics of family life.

If dreams are parts of behaviours built between us and ourselves, wounds are a "vivid" part of hurtful interactions with our parents and family members, in our early life and later with the outside world. People can afford to live with burdens, moving along the pathway of life with "up and downs". But when conflicts and troublesome experiences are frequent and distressing, life can become "hell". This is when psychotherapy becomes important if not necessary.

I don't have much experience with destructive personalities. Nevertheless I shall share the main aspects observed in my work. The following are fragments of sessions concerning some of the most disruptive and painful experiences for the developing structure of a child.

I shall use fragments showing that the experience of **"being ignored"** by significant others is disruptive. Experience shows how ambiguous such interaction is since ignoring is "passive aggressiveness". The adult has the power to "do or not to do". A child has no reaction to set on the field.

A fragment of a session with **Jane.**

In this session an unpleasant experience with her partner took her back to the destructive relationship in her early years.

Jane: *...I had a long, hard argument with David. He said he'd had enough. I thought, gosh! Now he is going to pack up and go away. For the first time I feared he was leaving.*

Th: *A scary feeling stirred up.*

Jane: *I felt abandoned.*

Th: *Does this scare you?*

Jane: *I am scared ... (silence) ...*

Th: *Can you see what it means to you? Do you feel in danger being on your own?*

Jane: *Yes. ...feeling like a little girl.*

Th: *You are a little child, powerless ... not enough strength (Personal Power) ... no one to help you ... fragile.*

Jane: *Yes, that's me. I remember when my mum would put me in the car, telling me she was taking me for a drive. I was happy because at home she usually ignored me... We were going somewhere... She had to meet a friend, she used to say, but she would leave me in the car and go off on her own with him. I used to feel unhappy and cheated.*

Th: *Something like abandoned... in the "nowhere"...*

Jane: *Now I understand why I need David. Why I am scared to upset him: if he gets angry and goes away, I am lost. I realize I never complained with my mother. I was scared she would ill-treat me... I would be lost.*

I noticed she suddenly cuddled up. Her arms around her body. I asked her....

Th: *What are you feeling?*

Jane: *I have the feeling of like... disappearing...*

Th: *Is this an old feeling?*

Jane: *Yes. If you speak to someone and this person ignores you... It is like disappearing... You don't exist.*

Th: *You feel lost "inside" yourself and "outside"...*

Jane: *Yes. It is a deliberate non-attention because when I was ill- treated I was suddenly visible.*

It is the **"inside" feeling of being lost, impotent thus in danger, thus scared,** that makes these people "disappear". Sometimes they say, "it's like falling into an abyss".

Maggy. (Encounter group)

Mag: *...In my family quarrels, disputes were endless. I was terrorized. I* *would feel my limbs being dismantled piece after piece. Like crumbling down ... coping with things too difficult for me to understand. Too threatening. I was only twelve years old. I would tell them to stop but nobody considered me. Now also, when there are disputes, I feel I'm crumbling. The blood disappears from my veins.*

Th: *It seems very scary...*

Mag: *Oh Yes!*

The way she said this gave me the impression she didn't even have the courage to say the word "scary". I saw her clenched fists, her body shrinking.

Th: *Seems that your power crumbles. The power that should react, crumbles. Your strength vanishes. Can you get deeper into this feeling of terror?*

Mag: *If I think of myself when I was a child, I get that feeling. Now, when I take a shower and water runs over my face I have a terror, like: now I can't defend myself: my strength is fading away... the water is going to defeat me...*

Once again, paralyzing terror of the past is the game.

A silent crushing. Dealing with inflexible judges

Betty

A young undergraduate student has the painful feeling of being scornfully ignored. She grew up in a family that never involved her in any kind of conversation or discussions. She was always second to a sister who had all the attention. The following is a clear glimpse of how interactions worked.

Betty: *When I go with them on holidays, if I happen to ask them (sister and brother in law) to stop because I saw something nice in a shop window or when driving through beautiful places, I ask to stop so we can take photos, there is no reply. They keep on going as if nobody spoke. If my sister asks the same things, her husband turns around and goes back. If we are in the car, he drives back even if it's only to take a shot of a tiny flower along the road. I don't exist. The most devastating feeling is of "disappearing". I disappear also to myself. (I-Me no longer exists).*

Th: *A feeling of* **"nothingness"**. *(Seeds of respect and dignity do not grow into life).*

Betty: *Yes ... It's like falling into a void...*

Th: *All this means you always hope they will listen to you. (The innocent child is craving the dream). Thus, there goes the feeling and need you have: to "belong to"...*

Betty: *...(Silence)... Yes... (Cries).*

- **As we can see, "needs-dreams" are stronger than**

"wounds"…

- Human destructiveness **"has no respect"** whatever.
- **Respect** "transcends" all limits. Our own, just as well as others'. It has to do with "unconditional regard". Lack of respect destroys the child's Self Concept, or image of oneself. Respect pertains to the philosophical concept of "limits". It is the border beyond which lies the Infinite. It is the freedom to act according to one's consciousness. Respect acts where my limit means respect toward you.
- The experience of **being the target** of non-respect is being suspended over a void. A disappearing. Energy dies out. The **tree of life** is at risk of drying out/dying.

The root of destruction

"If I killed all my emotions, don't you dare show me yours"…

Why? How can some people be so destructive? How come?

* In their life, there has been a "split".

* In their early experiences, they were also hurt and injured, many times **for no reason.**

* When innocently injured-damaged, the experiencing of loss-pain, (also physical) fear, deadly feelings, are **"relegated to silence".**

* The "sense of innocence", mortification and "fear", move to the "cognitive" level. Neuroscience could tell us how it takes place.

* The dialogue with feelings is "rejected" because they feel innocent and will not accept the "cruel reality" that they have "lost the game". Their **"innocent nature"** asserts its righteousness. This turns them into **merciless judges.**

THUS:

** Innocence goes to the cognitive level. It is a Rational Value. I am innocent. I have the "right" to receive caring, love and respect.

** Emotions: pain-loneliness-fear- at the mercy of powerful abusers- in deadly Traps-powerless- defeated, are all rejected emotions. Buried down in darkness. In the world of "still emotions".

** Loss. They have lost the game. A defeated feeling. Rejected into the deepest part of the Self and forgotten.

** Structure. They build a severe-strict - harsh structure: only black or white. No other way is accepted. When the structure is threatened, challenged in their minds, fear utters an unconscious sound and instead of fear, anger and violence appear. Biology would say **in their genes, there are no "variances".**

7 From the psychological void to philosophical void

"The finitude of being"

When psychology and philosophy intersect

*On the border of the silver threads **(Funerals)** stands the **pathway to the essence of "Existence".***

After having troubled/traveled so much to let go our dreams, after struggles to let go the silver threads, after having given up the strawberry ice creams, after having healed the wounds caused by our caregivers and that were bleeding so, after accepting the void, THE GREAT QUESTION arises: "AND NOW?"

A client asks "But, afterwards? ... What is left?... I am scared to discover that I've got nothing more".

When Rogers states that the actualizing tendency can be jammed, this means that behaviour (action) is incongruent with what is "felt". The "me". Frequently, it occurs that this defensive mechanism is unconscious and deeply hidden so as not to hear its cry. Consciousness of incongruent behaviour is often burdened with the "experiencing" of incongruent family dynamics.

The therapeutic process helps us to get rid of all this "trash" but afterwards we feel "naked" and on our own…

Let us see what a client says:

From a session

…I grew up with the firm belief inculcated by my family and by a strict catholic education, that nobody is perfect. Most of all, that I was not the perfect one. This went on until I stopped thinking myself as a small, poor, vacuous,

transparent, limited being, whereas, all others were people worthy of great consideration, important. They could **crush** *what I already had crushed: myself (the "me", the actualizing tendency)).*

The journey has been very long. At last, I began to think and feel like a person with positive aspects. The dimension and consideration of others decreases as the consideration for myself increases… Now, I am afraid… If I free myself from this…what have I of mine?…

The client is experiencing a feeling of fear together with desolation. It is comprehensible and in the order of things. It is an inevitable passage. Some clients clearly point it out: *"…before there was the purpose to* work *on my dreams… and now?… What can I do? …* **Where am I going?…**

The moment is extremely interesting for the therapist and for the client. It is the **prelude** for an important shift. In my experience, as a therapist, I noticed that once the battle comes to the end, and that is when we decide to cut the silver threads, we **get rid of our neurosis.** From an existential point of view, our neurosis did have an aim. It consisted of behaving "that way" in order to exist. Neurosis, after all, has been "a big job!"

When we realize we have been living for an "aim" and this aim no longer exists, that some patterns are inadequate for our actualizing tendency, there comes the feeling of not knowing where to go. It is a delicate moment. Sadness and melancholy for what has been comes welling up and there is uneasiness for what there is now. **It is a sense of "void". Another one!** It is no longer the void of our story, the void we have filled with its own void, but the **"true" void.**

This void represents the **void of the Being,** which is the **VOID OF EXISTENCE.** The feeling that nothing remains and has the sensation of going toward "nothing". However, something remains, **One Self.**

Let us see: illusions have crumbled. The neurotic work carried out so far has been emptied. What is this new feeling? What is happening? We realize that **"external values"** too are fragile, emptied of the investments made; they are precarious, limited, temporary, impermanent.

As we can see, now we are considering the **"external - universal values".** In a philosophical sense: values that are "of the world". External values also are precarious. **Existence has a beginning and an end.** Everything is precarious and impermanent. It is the **Great**

Truth. In a first moment, everything collapses again. We feel the "void of existence". It is **the Great Truth.** When we accept this philosophical concept, **"The Finitude of being",** we are **free.** We have nothing to lose.

The image given by Rogers, of the river, our story that flows toward the ocean of life and with which it will mingle and merge, is a good representation of this stage. We reach it only if we have walked all the way through our life history. We move from our Inner Values to Universal Values and accept them in their finitude/limits, just as we have accepted our inner limits: omnipotence against limits, thus wisdom.

The person regenerates with a new inner strength that is **Personal Power**, the **Consciousness of Limits.** Limits that have the meaning of acceptance of one's finitude and not the license for any kind of behaviour toward others.

Finitude of our "Being in the World"

Consciousness and acceptance of one's impotence is the link into the cycle of life, to giving birth and dying, to a sense of the **Finitude of Being.** It is a feeling of temporariness, precariousness enclosing the **concept of uncertainty or doubt about the reason for being.**

The last effort consists of getting over the anguish of this "nothingness". What is the reason for this life? Everything comes to "END". ...Is it so?... All this work, to get to this? ... This is the cry.

Whatever may be the answer, the **Constant** for any kind of answer is **"the end"** of this something that we are. We accepted the finitude of our personal inner world with its story. Of our Reality. Now we must accept the finitude of our "being in the world".

From nothingness to Freedom

The acceptance of our reality and our finitude leads to the acceptance, as far as possible, of **the concept of Death.**

** Death as an end, with the meaning of "nothingness".

** If we maintain the sensation of "nothing", this means, "there was something".

** Nothing implies "everything" or "nothing". Nothingness is an "absolute", once we accept deep down in our Soul/Self the concept that everything is limited and impermanent. There is but finitude and at this point, we feel that **** *There is nothing more to lose*.** The sensation inspired, is of **Freedom.**

The rhythm of life is now of the **"here and now".** Time is **"timeless",** because there are no longer eyes looking forward, into the future/dark. The past is no longer standing in front of us…and we flow into time and can appreciate "a blade of grass".

A blade of glass
and the Nothing…is Nothing
A silence and
inertness… are Nothing
Nothing can be something
Something does not exist because
Nothing or the absolute are the same
Be or not to be in this dimension
are the same thing.
Here or there
are equivalent.
From: A psychotherapy? No. A lifetime

From a session

Zephyrus: *"…I experienced a sensation of freedom, but do not understand where it is coming from, since I have nothing more to hang on to… I kind of… have nothing more to lose and I feel free…"*

Freedom is just another word
for nothing else to lose…
Janis Joplin

The time of "here and now"

Being in the "here and now" can be envisaged as a series of dots. Put in line they form an **Infinite line**. The "Being in the world" becomes a timeless being. The two ends: *"beginning"* and *"end"* meet in a being "without time". Thus, it is the end, that gives life to beginning in a **"timeless circle of life".**

Fragments of sessions
Carl

"…now, I clearly see everything down to the roots and say to myself: This is how things have gone and no other way. Reactions, solitude, misunderstandings, violence, no help to find my way when I was in high school. No time for me,

whereas I needed them in certain moments…to experience their closeness if I needed them. There are moments when I think back to all this and I sense the greatness of what I have been able to do in spite of the burdens of my wounds and voids, I am proud of how strong I have been…".

Carl was able to integrate into his inner Self the reality of his story. This was made possible only when he totally accepted "what has been" and went through all the suffering. There is a lot of sadness, for what happened, for what was done, for what he did to himself. Nevertheless, he has also been **resilient** since he succeeded in his profession.

Now his adult part, unchained from the past, is able to build emotional experiences allowing him to "go back" to that part of his history with the feeling of an indemnified pain and a strong feeling for the work he did. It is a real farewell to all "that has been".

Zephyrus

"…yes…it is time to lose omnipotence, but you find yourself with a great strength…Now while I am speaking I am putting pieces together of what I have been thinking in these days. The pleasure was great, but I also felt a sense of death… (silence)…yes now I understand… It was the sense of the limit and of the end…I am discovering that things have an end…I am discovering I can enjoy the pure taste of things. I clearly realize that they have an end. I went to Rome for the congress. For the first time, I enjoyed the city with a sense of freedom and full pleasure … but a feeling of void welled up…of death…yes, that's It…This void was different from other times…I was not able to explain …Now it is clear…the limit of things, the end of everything…I've got nothing more"…(silence)…I give a graft: "you remain"…Yes, it's true…I who am a catholic had never felt this so clearly.

Zephyrus went on making changes and considering the values of life; useless hopes. This is a clear demonstration of the shift from the feeling of void in one's *story*, to an *existential* void. It takes place only when we come to terms with the unsolved parts of the Self, with our conflicts, wounds healed, filled the inner void with its "experiential" feelings. Put an end to expectations and illusions. At this stage of the process, we face the "external void" that has to do with our "being in the world".

Once we have come to terms with the existential void, we feel the pure beauty of "Being".

The client adds: *"A **paradox** is that while on one hand, things lose their* *value, on the other hand they have another value…I feel a great strength, that I cannot call omnipotence… it is something different"*…(Silence) I say "do you mean that **now even a blade of grass has a value?"**. Her eyes shine up… *"Yes! That's it!"*

Zephyrus went on explaining to me, and to herself, changes in the perception of values, sterile investments and a new perception of many things.

It is a clear demonstration of the shift from the void pertaining to the inner world, towards something else: an "existential void". It appears to consciousness only when we have come to terms and closed "the game" with "unfinished business" of the Self. With our conflicts. Healed our bleeding wounds: filled the inner voids. Put an end to illusions. The "external void" pertains to "our being in the world". Once again, we see the step that follows: the **pleasure of "just Being"**.

As we can notice, there is often a repetition in pointing out the steps in the process. The intention is to show that step by step there is progress and shift from the inner world, representing **a history of life**, to an outside world that becomes a **philosophical point of view**. Transcending these values and dealing with "universal values" leads to a **"spiritual dimension"**. We shall consider these aspects in the last chapters.

Concept of feeling and nothingness

A pleasure for the therapist is, when the client puts the pieces of the puzzle in the right place, into the "inner Self", recognized as a piece of the Self.

Psychotherapy is a work of patiently putting pieces together. The pieces turn into the composition/picture of how "it **has been**" and of "what **has not been"**. Later, along the process with the aid of other pieces of the puzzle: the hidden ones, the distorted ones, we rebuild the "picture" that will show the "real meaning" of the story. There are examples of how sometimes we must give a different perception/meaning to a person's story. Maybe we need to have a clear idea of a few concepts.

Some clinicians from different lines of thought state: "what we do not experience, cannot be felt as "missing". The sense of "void" does not exist. Since we have no "knowledge", it cannot produce negative consequences. On the contrary, when we go and reassemble our story, we gain the consciousness of "white pages", "Missing" needs, the natural needs in the developing stages of life. (Maslow)

Existential Psychotherapy has the gift to offer the pathway to go back to those white pages, to find out what is "missing", to come to terms with the void, and fill the void with the ancient plaintive cry.

Here I shall briefly insert the **concept of "feeling" and of "nothingness"**. Some examples will specify the meaning.

Reading reality. Giving the right meaning to pieces of the puzzle

Here are examples of how sometimes we must give a different perception/meaning to a person's story.

Ann, age 61

"...the other day I understood that the core of the problem is that my mother always wanted me to assure her that everything was ok. If I fell sick, she would comfort me by saying that everything was all right... If my grandparents or my father or she herself fell ill, she would minimize the fact. The problem was that if I was **sick "inside",** *I didn't know how to explain it and couldn't find in her or in others, an interlocutor who would have ears for my inner pain. The point is that I have grown up incapable of sharing my afflictions".* Ann did have a need: a caring mother, but instead she was **"uncared for".**

Mary

"...I used to go to parties but I didn't exist... I was there but I didn't know what was going on. There was only fear...and "not being". In a deep part of me, there was a contact with the outside world, but unable to spring up and become an act of life. I had to learn on my own to stay with people...Now what I find is a wounded child, the one who was unable to cope with problems and who is carrying with her, also now, the experiencing of a "being in trouble" with the same patterns used to cope with those difficulties".

Later on in another session.

"...inside of me there is a **neglected** *child crying. She has been left alone, everyone has gone. There is no longer anybody for her. She looks around with eyes full of fear, and there is the dark. She retires into her shell so as not to see the dark and not to hear the silence".* When I experience love, at the same time I also feel the pain of these wounds: the **"missing"** is calling.

When Mary began her psychotherapy she came to my studio, "walking along walls" to feel protected...

Once that the adult part works on these wounded parts, the client is able to **give the right meaning to all these pieces of the puzzle.**

The inner child shall come out "from under the table" and bloom in the beauty of her essence: her Actualizing Tendency. Before reaching this stage, she has to go a long way. She has to deal with the fears that belonged to "real facts". **Fears and incomprehensible realities** she had to bury deep down in the darkness of a hidden world. Once she connects in touch with her inner child, the adult part will be able to experience the pain and fear of those days. A reality incapable to cope with. The adult part will say to the "confused" child that things went "that" way. The reality of her story. The story of a father closed in his own world and a mother overwhelmed with irrational fears. Before being able to feel and do this she *will have to say it* to herself and have the courage to feel and accept ... The "journey" has been very long. Her resistance in "protecting" her mother from any kind of "charges" (reading the crude reality), was strong. She had "very good reasons" for doing so. Was "saving" her mother from "leaving her at the mercy of herself" if she, Mary, had to change the "frame of reference". **Before "telling the true story" to her child (her inner part) she had to tell the truth to herself.** The adult part had to accept it first, in order to be able to offer to be a "brink to lean over". Saying this to herself, she will feel all the pain, the anguish of *being all alone at the mercy of herself;* **there were no caregivers. The confusion** between what Mary was experiencing, the reality Mary was reading and the reality mother was describing. From this contact, this "experiencing", springs a feeling of strength (see Zephyrus). Will contact the fear, the chagrin, but at length from the contact grows the feeling of a restored "dignity".

In my experience I've noticed that when clients hold on to a BIG LIE, that they are trying to save at all costs, the "distorted reality" is that they must desperately "SAVE" the careless caregiver (They feel they are condemning them) because, when they CUT the thread "holding them together", they will "crumble" and get lost...

The whole process conveys an important concept. When it comes to end, we must become aware in our inner Self that **"We have lost the game". We've lost the game "because we are impotent". We must "give up" to reality.** Another tough moment is, when we stop bearing illusions and cut our silver threads, a feeling of total loneliness creeps in. It is inevitable because we have always been accustomed to be "hanging" on to something or someone. Now we are **alone....** With ourselves.

I want to point out that children afraid of the dark or of "the black man" actually bear within them a much bigger fear: **Being "Alone" in the "world",** without adequate means/tools. Incapable of facing the world, because a minimum of *"Landmarks/points of reference" are missing.* Without the most important feeling for a child: the protection of a caregiver. *"How can the child build safe "inner security" if the outside world is not providing safe experiencing?"* This aspect of being alone and of loneliness is the next to consider.

A Poem

Oh please my little child
don't laugh, no don't laugh, I pray you
Oh, No! Don't laugh anymore, my dear child
I beg you…
No more must you hide my dear child
your sorrow, your shame
innocent
behind your beautiful smile.
The Masters of power
are not worthy
of your sweet smile.
Come, I shall take you far away with me
where you shall be able to laugh and laugh
in the wind of freedom
that shan't ever hurt you.

From: A psychotherapy? No… A lifetime

The world of feelings

The world of feelings is not always easy to reach. It is, however, the most important part of Client Centred Therapy. All the aspects of our story need intellectual work, but feelings and emotions carry out the most important part of a therapy. Recent studies conducted by neuroscience confirm that every behaviour (existential act) originates from feelings and emotions.

Emotions lead to deeper levels of consciousness and allow certain aspects to be considered from different angles or enable us to move down to deep and hidden parts of the Self. Usually, at the first level or stage of the process, the client explains at a low emotional level. Only after some time we get in touch with reality and realize/understand how things really are and how they were in the past. This is the pathway leading to the emotional world of the past: emotions and experiences that we neglected and hid. Our structure and behavioural patterns can change only when we change the feelings and emotions pertaining to our conflicts, frustrations, fears, loss and so on.

What remains is only "me"

"Being alone" is not to be confused with a child *"being alone/neglected"* when left alone. It is being alone due to a choice. It is an autonomous entity. It appears after cutting the strings that kept us tied to others. This kind of "alone" cannot and must not be experienced by a child, since it is incapable of being autonomous by nature.

It is not even the **"neurotic being alone"** linked to the dream and still in need of someone else to lean on.

This is a client saying … *it is a … I am on my own… I have cut everything … got rid of all my abusers. What I had always been searching/craving for has crumbled. That sense of existence, the importance of values …I no longer perceive them in the same way. Now they have no value. Maybe in the end, what remains is… yes … I - AND MYSELF.*

The client takes about fifteen minutes to work this out. She spent many months working on **"being alone"… and "being without a sense".**

A poem
We are quick with our minds
Too fast in thoughts and recollections.
Slow in feeling our hearts
our emotions
what remains of our adventure
of a reality fading in colours.
Weighed down by the domination of reason
the tam-tam of feelings
comes little by little but already slips away.
The shell of our body
swiftly overtakes us
and the more sensitive antenna
are reduced

to firm and motionless sculptures,
beautiful, shiny, coloured
wonderful to see
nevertheless useless.
The form, the actions, the thought
useless shield of the world
where beauty and happiness
are impalpable
and moved by incomprehensible strings.
The mystery however
is what makes us move.
(A client)

How slow the moving on

Let us follow Anny's Moving along. These are fragments of writings.

"*So far I never behaved according to my ideas but to suggestions given by others who are not me or that I still dare not call by name. I know that this will go on for some time and that so far I cannot behave otherwise. In these recent days, I happened to understand that things have gone exactly this way. Now words can explain things: multiform and ambiguous. Whereas I wish, at least, they could easily and immediately tell me how physical the event is. How tangible the inner dimension is*".

Later, she writes:

"*I would never have been able to do all this on my own. There have been two of us right from the beginning. Right from when I started out. (Therapy). There were also two of us when I could not "Be" if not with a very small part of me. I can see how much Maddalena, from the very first day, has been present and capable at the same time, leaving the space I was in integral. Integral has often the meaning of "nearly empty"; sometimes occupied by something twisted, frightened, in pain. Words that often expressed the inability to say, or voice the need to hinder. It's only now that I realize how invasive she could have been and the difficulties she could have added to those already existing. She could have been a person incapable of respect or a person who had not gone deep down into herself for a long time before moving into another's ocean*".

8 Where psychology meets philosophy

The process of revival and back into the world. A psychological point of view

So far, we have walked along the pathway of our story to recover our **Actualizing Tendency** and live according to our potentialities and **talents.**

The first feeling, back in the world, is of "nothingness". Silver threads used to make our dreams come true are no longer there. Omnipotence and Magic Ideas give way to Wisdom. Once we come to terms with our Inner nothingness, the **Existential Nothingness** appears. The nothingness of "Being". A reality of our "being" in the world with all its limits. The limits of "humanity": the **Impermanence** of its values and the material world.

The great secret of life is that life has no sense if not the sense WE give it. Friedrich Nietzsche in his famous book "Zarathustra" says: *Behave as you are. In order to give the right sense to life, we must be alone in our solitude. Accept the limit of life, which is death.*

Be-coming is "evolving," keeping all the pieces of the Self together. We can regard it as one's solar system; without exploding or imploding. Since we are reflecting our Personal Light, we ourselves are "the light" and are clearly visible from outside. This solar system will finish with us when we get to THE END of our existing "in the world".

We cannot embrace the philosophy of Globalism using the language of Positivism and Structuralism. It would create the chaos of Babel. It is impossible to have an exchange between psychic and mental spheres.

He who explains the concept of freedom without considering the boundaries of another person, is not living in the dimension of the "being" pertaining to existential philosophy.

When I use my freedom according to the frame of relativity, (the relativity of things) my behaviour ends on the border where the freedom of someone else begins. That border is for me my limit, but also my infinite. It is an "Infinite" understood as "living with others in the world", that is "Mit-Sein" or "With-Being".

I determine my infinite as regards my need, the "FIGURE", that will never be absolute and unconditional. It is conditioned by the consciousness of **belonging**, or being in the world **with others.** This determines the "BACKGROUND". Thus, my *need and my limit* determines the *infinite.* (Nothingness/Absolute). The difference lies in man's psychic conception. I perform my relativity when I connect with you. Here the universal value of "Respect" is in action. **Respect is nothing but a pure act of consciousness. Then, I open on to the INFINITE with you.**

Those who live in the Positivist schema which sets limits (being a definite structure), perceive their personal sphere as "definite", whereas for the existentialist it is "indefinite". Positivism is in the same dimension as experimental Physics, "foreign" to the concept of the psyche peculiar to Rogerian psychology: Finitude/Nothingness.

As long as we remain in the schema of also "quantifying" relativism, this means staying in the positivist framework. Dialogue becomes "dispersive". Positivists consider whatever is not verifiable devoid of sense. They do not consider the relativist dimension of things.

He who states that truth does not exist, (Nihilism) thus believing he is free from schemas, still moves within the dimension of Positivism. This involves always keeping a distance. He who is in the dimension of existential psychology does not even see it as a problem.

If I say that truth does not exist, this means that I ASK myself if it exists. He who states that truth does not exist, is the same person who denied or is denying what he previously believed. For he who lives in the dimension of Relativism the fact that truth exists or not, is of no importance.

Whatever element is extrapolated from its "whole" becomes a

Figure, but cannot lose its identity as to *"that"* whole, which becomes its BACKGROUND.

If we do not stay anchored to "that background", the figure can become everything …and nothing. Thence, I am in a state of "dispersion".

On the contrary, if we examine figure A on a background B not pertaining to A, it can create a misunderstanding.

The perception of reality from a structural point of view differs from a relativistic point of view: one is "freedom **from** a schema," the other is "freedom **in** its "being".

One has its maximum limit in the infinite that goes beyond the borders that limit it, the other has its maximum limit…in *nothing, because there is nothing beyond itself.*

The freedom to "spit out whatever" to someone else "because this is what I want/desire" is a freedom in "dissoluteness". True freedom is that of self-control and if I live in "true and real" contact with myself, I shall never need to spit over anyone.

Thus, we come to terms with **the first concept of existentialism** and **the first universal value** that says "An existential act is nothing but a **PURE ACT OF CONSCIOUSNESS.** The first value in consciousness **is RESPECT.**

There where the narrator is faithful, eternally, inflexibly faithful to his story, there, in the end, silence speaks. There, where the story is betrayed, silence is just a void.
KAREN BLIXEN.

NEVER FORGET
WHERE YOU COME FROM
OTHERWISE
YOU WILL NEVER KNOW
WHERE TO GO

Madeline Bosio.

Conclusion

On concluding this work, my deep hope is that what remains impressed is the strength of all the evidence given by the life story of my clients.

They are a precious, unique patrimony that no theory can give. It helps to think over one's own life story. A hint, to those who do this work, to give a scientific contribution... provided phenomenology can be "contained" into something systematic... I admit I have not been able to do so.

I chose to share some moments of my "intimate" life as a psychotherapist, because I believe that giving voice to one's experiences is more effective than any theoretical treatment.

It is in this "nuance" that I intend to conclude my work. Through a letter from Zephyrus.

"Today I crumbled, literally shattered. Better still, I stopped keeping these clothes already long in tatters, tied together, with a titanic and useless effort. I do not know for how long. Maybe since I was wearing that little dress, once white, but now worn out and gray and I found myself on my own. In front of me, many roads. A few days ago, I found some old photos of myself in that dress. I was about five years old. I wanted to bring it to you, but forgot it. These days, when I'm with my mother, or when, rarely, I meet my sister-in-law, or my brother, or my nephews, whose punishment I received, though it didn't have a name then, I interpret the past, recall memories and little by little I now understand. Nevertheless, I can't understand why my mother ignored me and keeps on ignoring me. If she had "hated" me openly (to make an absurd hypothesis), perhaps she would have left me free to be myself. Instead she always insinuated herself into me

with mechanisms instilling guilt, along with complete indifference. This kind of relationship clearly became the way I "let others" relate to me. The reason is that so far I don't know any other way. Now I seem to be, I feel like a little girl, looking for "someone" to take her by the hand. That little girl was in the dark. For a short time, "that someone" was my "second" mother. A dear woman: my next- door neighbour. It is hard to say...for many years I had been alone, waiting, until one day we met. At once, I felt a strong attachment. I tried to control it, because I perceived a sensibility, interest, respect, towards me that puzzled me. When I told doctor Rossi "she loved me", I believed it and I still believe so, even though I am conscious of both our roles. I understand I must find those sentiments toward Zephyrus "in me" but they do not exist, or better, they are hidden, dormant, and I am upset but astonished, at finding them in another person. Anyhow, this tells me they are sentiments that do exist and can become mine or that I can awaken them. I would like to gain respect and sense of dignity. Not even a friend can make you have these feelings within yourself, especially if you didn't have such experiences with your parents. I could have called these sentiments "love for oneself", but I feel it's too vague; pride is better. That is what I was saying before: respect for myself, and my dignity. I am starting to have these feelings through her. I am starting... behind me I have a story that is turning out so devastating that I am only just starting to think of myself in terms that are not scornful. It is not easy nor automatic. When I think I have understood, I discover thousands of other negative attitudes towards me. Never before had I thought about the feelings of Zephyrus toward Zephyrus. I never thought about Zephyrus, I was secondary even to myself. Transparent...or tapestry; depending on the situation. At present, for many, I am still tapestry. My mother is amongst these: it couldn't be otherwise. I am now becoming conscious of the horror. I now understand denial, and that "I was educated to deny myself". I don't know what else to say. I am feeling "annals" of tiredness..."cosmic". All evening I have been shedding tears, but am not in desperation. Today, Madeline, when you talked to me about my frailty, I saw myself very well and clearly. I now recall a situation, a little bit comical, but this helps me not to give it a dramatic twist. I am thinking of imprinting and of me as a duckling eventually coming out of the shell and luckily finding the "right duck" to follow. Just as well, it was not a cat! I am sorry I never paid for the sessions I missed. I was not aware, even if you had noticed it. I apologize I didn't ask you today but I was upset, a duckling in a stormy sea, very stormy...".

When I had the "first session" with Zephyrus, I did not inform her that sittings missed were to be paid. In front of me I had a creature who was so devastated and "crushed" that another "weight" to shoulder … was too much for the "little inner child" I saw in her…

That day during the sitting, I had given her feedback of her "being in frailness". The therapy had been going on for a few years.

From a client
For Madeline
Thank you for calling me friend
For being there when we travelled
In the Netherlands of
Warped pain and refusal
When your face would hit doldrums
When I saw reflected there
The nothingness I couldn't escape
Thank you for holding me
And crying with me
When the realest pain
I'd ever known ripped me apart
Leaving me empty but calm
Thank you for being my friend and sister
For unmasking your Australian Self
Just long enough
For me to see
The warm fury koala bear in you
Thank you.
An English client.

At the end of a course specializing in Clinical Sexology, a student hands me the following writing.

"With infinite affection and deep gratitude for having "guided" me so far".

I AM READY

I don't know,
I don't know what this void is
I don't know
I don't know why… one day…is no longer enough
I don't know why this fear
This mad fear to lose everything
I do not know.
How hard it is, to look into eyes
Those ghosts without a face and without a name:
Searching amongst those crumpled sheets
of one's story
what an effort!
I hear him inside, that child screaming with fear.
I would like to take his hand
but thence I do not know.
I do not know how much his wounds are still bleeding.
But it is no longer enough, no longer enough
to play loud music,
surrounded with friends, love with all my soul
with the illusion it shall never end.
I do not want illusions.
I need silence.
I need to listen to that scream
cuddle that child.
I don't want a movie,
I want my life.
And… another story starts again.

The paradox of the wise Buddha

"To live and be free we need to know we are mortal; to know we are mortal we must have gained consciousness of our immortality, of the here and now that inspires the sense of without time".

As we can see, the "Invisible Lines" guiding the big picture …are all the same…

WHAT IS LIFE? WHO ARE WE?
*** Quantic theory states:**
"We are pure energy". Thus, death gives us back to "eternal cosmic life".
*** We then ask the question: "Is it spiritual"?...**
"The answer my friends is blowing in the wind"...
(Bob Dylan)

Part 2

Sexual abuse in childhood

Recurring emotional experiencing in clinical work with adults

"The way out is through"

9 Abused women in childhood and abusers

The work I have been doing with women sexually abused in childhood, has given me the opportunity to figure out some important aspects in the healing process as regards victims and to try to find the roots of violence as regards abusers.

These observations need further clinical research, even though I consider them important since they stem from a **"phenomenological approach"**. The approach differs from others since it does not rely on any kind of theory, but goes deep into the client's experiential world. Specifically incest is a highly threatening experience for the Self Esteem a child has to build, in order to be able, in the future, to move in the world with confidence and respect towards oneself and the others.

It is the **"Existence" of the self**, in the philosophical sense, that is at risk, because the "Being" is undermined. Behavioural disorders, their complexity and extension, vary according to the age of the victim, relationship with the abuser or the kind of damage.

The aim of this study is to help operators who deal with abused adults or children.

I've identified **the principles underlying the outcomes** of the most painful disruptions a person might go through both on the interpersonal and affective levels, severely testing the personality structures. The principles I am going to describe are the outcome (with a high frequency) of psychotherapy with adults abused in childhood and who were compelled to come to terms with experiences buried deep inside but that kept on causing troubles in their lives. Precious material comes up from the depths of the victims' wounds. These are victims who survived their trauma.

The therapeutic process is always very slow and often causes despair since acceptance of the "chain" of realities, unfolded from dark corners where they had long been stored, is something like dying to oneself.

A healing therapy with children is different but the wounds are the same as those healed in adults.

I have also worked with abusive mothers, and women attracted by other children. The wounds are actually the same… Nevertheless there is a difference: there are specific aspects during the experience that diverge toward different behaviours.

The therapeutic target is to **recover Personal Power** by going through a process of acceptance. By going through the fear of being left alone; the terror of being at the mercy of oneself, experiencing the lack of defensive instruments; realizing that there were not adequate personal resources, while facing and coping with experiences so far from the victim's reality.

Clinical experience indicates that **terror rather than pain** is the mainspring for the recovery of one's personal power and ability to judge. Terror leaves many traces in adulthood and sometimes turns into violence. Experiences of family abuse throw the growing person into an affective dimension mainly marked by ancestral fear. It is similar to the experience an infant goes through the moment he comes to life and has to learn to breathe.

Uncertainty, ambivalence and perversion profoundly undermine two basic developmental elements:

- Judgement ability. That is to learn the difference between what is right and what is wrong.
- Empathy. Empathy leads to the control of violence. It helps to recognize and feel one's own pain as well as that of others and gives rise to an action or to control towards the world.

De Zulueta (1993) and Alice Miller (1988) point out that every violent behaviour, every impediment to emotional worlds has its roots in a past history of losses, betrayals, abandonment, neglect and in the anger that is produced, an anger that doesn't allow to recognize, hence connect with one's feelings.

My clinical experience suggests that behind a painful feeling, more than anger, there is a **hidden terror.**

An important aspect to bear in mind:
** Anger is a feeling towards the "other": I – thou. Terror is a feeling that belongs to the "self": **I-me.** (Buber Martin.)

** There is fear that appears the moment when the child senses it is without protection.

** There is the child's fear to lose the figures that are its reference-points. At the same time the child is helpless. Terror destroys and distorts the affective potential of the growing person.

** Cognitive process is also severely compromised, because there is the failure to handle and understand what is really happening. *The unknown becomes fear.*

** Fear, as usually occurs in panic experiences, **breaks down** the cognitive and emotional functioning plunging the victim into a dark prison of ambivalence. This concept has recently been confirmed by Neuroscience.

** Last but not least, terror springs from the endless, unbearable feeling of being left alone... lost in the world... **Being in Loneliness**

** In the case of a **breakdown** of the defensive system, **terror turns into violence** and often perversion.

10 Disruptive experience

Terror dismantles the "structure of existing"

It is important to consider several aspects of the Ego, involved in this dramatic experience, in order to be able to help the survivor to recover after the shattering experience.

I found two important nucleus that I consider the **PILLARS** from which all other aspects of the abused child, and later the adult, radiate: **Power and Being that will affect Existing**.

On one hand, there is an *"abuse of power"* by the adult, on the child.

On the other, there is an "expropriation" and thus the *shattering of "being"*, in the victim.

When the abuser is also a parent, this causes further, far more serious problems since incest is the most serious of taboos ever existing. The victim is unable to confront the event with any other kind of experience. It is in itself a behaviour considered "against nature".

A good number of **Personal Constructs get turned upside-down.** Survivors have a feeling of violation, or being victims of a robbery, cheated by those who were supposed to protect and defend them and offer unconditional love.

During psychotherapy with adults, the therapist tries to produce a Personal Construct: the basis for "stems" that will re-build self-esteem. Something like skin reconstruction on a body damaged in an accident.

Their experience is like having been in a "deadly" place where they came out "alive" (in the words of a client). Abuse is an experience that **carries within itself the taste of death**:

** Death in a relationship with a parent.

** Death of trust in other people and in a world that many times does not believe the victim.

** Death in the moment of the shattering of the powerless and lethally wounded self.

** It is the death of one's "being in the world": "...*I feel uninhabited*" – "...*I feel devastated* ..." It is a Wasteland feeling.

**Death coming from the fear of being alone at someone's mercy; no protection. It is through this fear that the quality of "being" in terms of "Existing" undergoes a modification.

All these feelings inevitably summon TERROR.

One of the personal constructs I use, maybe the most significant, is the following: *"They have been in a place where not even angels dare to go". They came out alive...* There is no precise moment to use it. Only empathy and sensitivity can spot the right moment. It is like starting out on a long journey in order to repair what happened.

For the time being, this personal construct takes the place of "being in pieces". It is accepted like a *delicate caress,* maybe the very first one laid on so much havoc and will enhance the survivors' recollections and integration of the experience.

The Psyche undergoes a similarly schizophrenic trauma, since the victims often talk about having the feeling that the body is in one place, the story in another, while they are somewhere else.

WORK:

The work consists of putting these parts together again. We shall see this later. These intense experiences responsible for undermining the personality are described without a precise guideline. There are no guidelines even though in psychotherapy there is a "bundle" that gets untangled. There is an "approach code" for the things to be faced and it changes from person to person. I believe that this method is also useful for children.

There are sessions when the client keeps repeating the same topic, as if that were the most important aspect of the whole story. Of course there is an underlying meaning to all this. Other times it may happen that the incredulity is overwhelming. We must keep in mind that these people are a handful of "clots of blood" stored up inside in confused ways. The outline comes out as soon as the pieces of the puzzle are "faced and cleared".

The pieces of the puzzle

Now I shall point out some of the main pieces of the puzzle that need to be "gathered" during the healing process.

Piece A: **ROBBED**

A widespread concept of the experience is that of "**being robbed**".

Very first: children robbed of *"TRUST"*. Trust betrayed and betrayal has taken place in a particular sphere such as sex. Thus, it is a double betrayal. This leads them to have little or no trust in others.

"LIVING SPACE" violated and robbed. There has been a violation of the "borders" of one's "being a person". Borders that cannot be trespassed on. Not even by a parent, even though we often hear a parent say "Since I made you I can just as well destroy you…".

The abusive act deprives the child of a *"PERSONAL SENSE OF CONTROL"* of its own world, instead causing a feeling of impotence, of an inability to protect personal space.

The "safety space" between child and parents is very small and it is from this **violated space** that defensive mechanisms spring up, in an attempt to create a "big" safety space. In this case, the defensive system consists of keeping everyone at a distance. For example, there are abused mothers who cannot even bear a hug from their children. Only when they grow up, there can be a little change.

Others go through sexual intercourse with a feeling of "not being" *"…yes my body is there, but it's as if I'm not there…"* In other words, they do not exist in the relationship.

Others spread out too much with everybody; there are no more boundaries. This behaviour leads to their having sex on any occasion, in an unending experience of powerlessness and of possession of their body by another person.

Otherwise, again owing to this violated space, everything gets so messed up, that in an extreme attempt to save itself in an experience that cannot be faced, or handled, the victim "gets rid of the Being: a part of the Self is shifted (there is a split) in order to be able to forget. In this case, we are dealing with a Psychotic Defensive Trauma.

Nevertheless, eyes and body will never forget. Even though hidden in the depths of the body, the wounds will keep on bleeding until they are healed.

The therapist cannot get into this space using an assertive method, or following his/her own pattern or working programme. We can only accept and respect the distance decided by the client, who deep in his/her heart is aware that it is necessary to come to terms with **something desperately rejected.**

It will be the message that "we know where they have been. That it is a place from where they came out alive"; it will be this walking side by side that turns out to be the key that will open the way to a slow though painful recovery of personal power.

It is necessary to go through deep work regarding the fear of having been left alone and powerless – the specific feeling that comes from an absolute impossibility to cope with such experience of abuse – the failure to ask for help, to be able to give voice to fear *–to acknowledge the sexual experience* - to accept this reality.

Piece B: **INNOCENCE**

The victims are robbed of their innocence and with this word, I do not mean a moral value, but a feature that along with many others, is part of the child's developmental process. Innocence is a part of the child's identity, but after an experience of abuse a "confused" identity takes place… "*…against my will I became a grown up…*".

All this results in a **feeling of something very bad**, but of which one cannot grasp the meaning.

On a phenomenological level, the experience has **destroyed the sense of trust** (something is wrong, but I don't understand what) and the feeling of **being safe,** in other words, the warm feeling of protection.

This is an important aspect in perverted peoples' experience. We shall examine this later.

When violence goes through the "life space", the child is deprived of the feeling of CONNECTING, as in "It is me…" In other words, something has come "unstuck". The "grounding" feeling is damaged.

The frightful experiencing is made of "being utterly powerless" on one hand and on the other hand, there is an inconsolable pain growing from the sensation of "wreckage" into which the victim sinks… A feeling in which it is almost impossible to remain without risk for mental health.

The trauma is experienced with "eyes of innocence", and these eyes are often used when relating with others. This is an important aspect of the Short Circuit.

Sometimes, in the sessions, the sound of a child's cry produced by these adults is very disturbing.

In this whole scenario, the only one who remains clear headed is the abuser who, once more, has exorcized or reiterated something belonging to his/her own story. However, this scenario makes us realize that the beautiful "age of innocence" has been disrupted.

Piece C: **VIOLENCE**

When in addition to such events there is also violence, the victim behaves like a Vietnam survivor who recollects and again feels the pathos, the terror, the pain and the drama of his experience. At the same time, he feels and reports his enemy's violence that broke through *his shattered defensive system.*

The self is at risk of dissolving in this "switching" over from one person to the other. The feelings of "being" the victim are penetrated by those of the violent enemy… and the two figures are confused and interwoven in the victim's mind. At this point, also "existing" is at high risk: its STRUCTURE is in danger since at this point there are no adequate instruments. There is no functioning Personal Power.

This means that the defensive system is undergoing a severe trial, that the Self is struggling in an attempt to maintain a separation from the Other Self: at that moment, there is only powerlessness, a violent and unacceptable reality and feeling of being in "ruins". There is the **annihilation of "Being"**. Terror springs up; the cognitive world is useless, not functioning. It is here that the abuser's violence overcomes the victim's Self.

As I said before, **it is terror that "breaks" the defensive system of the Self.**

As long as the Self salvages some feelings, it will be safe. By contrast, when the Self is overwhelmed by the two parts clinging on to each other, the victim is doomed to repeat its own story "in the guise of the abuser". Is this a continuous "acting out"? This is the transition **from fear to violence**. We shall see how it works further on.

Piece D: **FEAR**

During the healing process, the work dealing with impotence and annihilation will enhance the connection with other feelings of pain and fear and therefore one feels the devastation of being and the terror for being so alone and hopeless while all this was taking place.

From the report of a survivor in adolescence

...The moment of the violence, is the first, total striking moment of awareness of being alone in that havoc. For two very simple though devastating reasons.

A person who has not undergone abuse can have no idea of what means to be within two boundaries: a physical one, and now I mean the body as a whole, and a spiritual one and I am talking about the energy each "Self" contains in order to assert its "Being".

When violence is taking place every nerve, every muscle, every cell of the body seems to amplify their sensations as if to rebel or to put the mind on the alert about what is taking place. The outcome is even more devastating. You've never felt your legs such a part of you, never had such a clear realization of how they "belong" to you. Your skin captures and remembers every chafing, every bruise with utmost precision and reluctant intenseness. Your hands understand their real purpose, their real power because it is of these two qualities that they are being robbed.

Then, you also understand the meaning of being a body in your inside, that you exist wherever there is flesh of yours, because every bit of flesh, even the part you have never touched, is crying and screaming its own "Being". That moment is the only one when silence would have been the best choice in front of the total impotence in that violent speechless statement.

Every cell, every nerve calls the mind and it is there that you gain the absolute certainty of **"being" in that guise, all over**. *Everywhere so powerless...*

You never ever had such a clear perception of yourself, except in that very moment when all what we had understood and found out about ourselves was taken away..."

Piece E: **A STOLEN CHILDHOOD**

If we go back to the period when these things were going on, we can figure out how the adolescent's' Self was too frail to cope with this kind of emotions, undoubtedly not typical at that age. We can understand the great struggle to avoid such a reality.

In other words, since the child had no adequate instruments, she was compelled to submit to reality instead of coping with it. The final act is a stolen childhood.

Piece F: **SHORT CIRCUIT** in the trauma

In family situations where there is a high amount of violence, it is clear how the child builds up "short circuit" mechanisms. There is:

** Waiting time

** Storming time

** Final act, when violence takes place, but that turns immediately into another repetition

** Waiting time…

This is what Michaela, a client who underwent physical and sexual abuse, says:

"…There wasn't a time that could have been called respite, because also silence had a noise, since I was already on the alert, waiting for the violence to be repeated (physical) because I never knew how, why, or when it was going to happen. Also the abuse was an uncertainty, since my father could grab me when I was on the sofa in the sitting room, when I was in bed, either alone or when there was my mother…".

Because of these experiences, communication and socialization get ever more difficult. It is unavoidable that these mechanisms go along with behaviours that express uneasiness, agitation, violence and closure. Michaela was ever more withdrawn; her behaviour was that of a silent docile girl who did not want to socialize with children of her age. When grown-up she had built a confused personality. From the social, sentimental and sexual point of view, she gave herself to everybody.

We can thus state that when there is an abuse of power, the child is not able to rebel and reject because the experience is painfully lived in utmost loneliness and fear. "On the stage" there are no reference points to rely upon. Her defence mechanisms are inadequate.

The situation is worse when parents try to get rid of any kind of responsibility by "blaming" the child.

Sandra experienced a situation of abuse up to her late adolescence when she found the courage to say to her father *"I don't want you to do those things to me"*…and her father answered: … *"why? …I thought you liked it…"*

In this case, also, there is a short circuit and it is hard for a child to stop it without somebody's help. The victim's experiencing is of the kind: who is the victim? Who is the abuser? Am I a victim? An abuser? Perhaps I am a party to all this? Besides these thoughts there are ideas of one's possibility of intervention like: "…I could have told him before…I could have stopped the thing…"

Is it our fault? (continues: the report of an adolescent)

"…One of the reasons why the fault is turned upon ourselves is that when we are alone, with the memories of the moment when we felt we were stolen away, the picture of what happened gets clear and complete all of a sudden, for a moment, an instant of total obscene awareness. There is nothing that can make us accept that we permitted the person in the picture to undergo such a violent deprivation…"

"There is a solution, when we think that we ourselves permitted it, maybe just a second, or a month earlier, with a look, a gesture that was certainly misunderstood. We should never had allowed it, they must have misunderstood, they have mistaken but it was us first of all who weren't clear…"

"There is so much violence inside of us that when we take in a bit of fault, this makes us feel a little stronger because, if it was really our fault, well…then tomorrow or within a month we will be able to avoid it. If it is our fault, well then we have the power "not to make it happen anymore…"

We have learned that the "illusion" of finding love is the thing that condemned us, and maybe this new illusion of a fault so impossible and not convincing, will save us.

Thus, they also have the illusion that they have solved the problem. The Short Circuit will "betray" this illusion.

These convictions are possible because there is lack of the dignity and pride that have the power to mark the boundary between the two "Beings". They are two aspects of personality that the child has not yet acquired. **The small amount of dignity and pride** so far structured, is trampled on by the abuse.

A result of what has been described is the following experience: *"this keeping oneself separate from the other person is impossible, so, I the victim, slip into the weird world of the other"*… because … the other person is the King of weirdness and flattery, because the other remains, beyond anything else, a Parent. (Incest)

Piece G: **COLLOCATION**

There is another frustrating aspect: the COLLOCATION of the experience because it does not belong to the child's sexual sphere, since it has not yet completely developed.

Here I ask myself why Freud thought that, though on an

unconscious level, the child's *Oedipal desire is satisfied*. (De Zelueta).

Through a slow and painful HEALING process, when the abused person is able to "take in" all this, it means that the "black hole" is reached. The client comes to terms with **that reality** and recognizes that what happened belongs to the inner world and accepts it as an identification of part of life and is impossible to erase.

Piece H: **FEELING "DIFFERENT"**

This is the reason why abused women feel they are "different" from others.

Thus, here there is another big obstacle to overcome, because before the acceptance of this reality, there is the upsetting feeling of being diverse. … *"At school I used to look around and ask myself if others could notice what was happening to me. Other times I would ask myself what my school friends' fathers might be like…."*

It is impossible to comfort them by saying that it is not true. This is one of the greatest griefs, since this being "different" carries along other feelings: *"…now I ask myself what kind of sexual life I would have had in adolescence if this hadn't happened…"* and so on.

In psychotherapy the work on these feelings and others, such as terror, sorrow, guilt, mourning, betrayal, painful cries, angry weeping also against the therapist, slowly gives way to grief for the "losses"; to the consciousness that they were victims of a taboo (in case of incest), and of its violence. It is a very tough and slow process of emotional holding.

It is not only a matter of getting clients to talk about the event. The work consists in walking with them into their **emotional world.** It is there that changes can take place. When they have the courage to experience, accept and take in the relinquished part of them, "the trauma", with the stigma of "being different" they come to feel a sense of INNOCENCE, a paradoxical process within the phenomenal method and closely adhering to the client's frame of reference.

It is the *"different one"*, who was betrayed. It is the *"different one"*, who has been in a place, where not even Angels dare go. It is the *"different one"*, who has been carrying a trauma.

The reborn feeling of innocence gives way to the feeling of being a *special person* because they have survived and can go proud of the fact that from that "black hole" they succeeded in coming out "by themselves". Now they are able to redeem the once rejected experiences and heal the Self, with all its no longer bleeding wounds, that nevertheless will always show the scars. **EXPERIENCE IS REDEEMED.**

Throughout all the therapeutic process, there is an everlasting "string". It is the feeling of "being left alone". The therapist must avoid the mistake of somehow replacing the "missing caregiver" (there is a VOID there…) or giving the protective feeling of a substitute for "what has not been". The client must have the feeling of you there as one who looks and reads with "eyes of Reality", who understands and accepts, who is confident, able to wait and respect, who suffers "with", but not "for".

The "trauma" I have described concerns the sexual event. Neuroscience confirms that the traumatic event, if not treated, gives way to a reiteration. A Short Circuit. We know that if we experience an earthquake, for a long time, we keep on observing if the light in the kitchen is swaying. Just seeming to sense something swaying, and terror comes into our eyes. Time can help to get back a feeling of safety. Catastrophic events require psychological help. The same concerns sexual abuse. Besides the "event" in itself, there has been a serious injury/disruption as regards the personality. It is a different kind of short circuit, because it has to do with an "uncompleted existential act".

The work on this aspect is in progress and will be published very soon.

11 The developing process to understand some aspects

We know that during emotional development, children are self-centred. They view the world from a subjective point of view and believe that everybody sees the world with the same eyes as them.

They feel all-powerful, but also guilty. They might believe that the negative aspect in the family is their fault. It is possible because they still have a magic thought: *"I haven't done…I failed… I could have"*…and so on.

External values internalized become part of their world: *"This is not to be done…This is bad…"* and so on.

Owing to these **internalized values,** the abused child feels something "doesn't fit". Things concealed. He/she has the sense of something threatening.

Since the child is unable to keep the Self distinct from the other, it says that it's his/her fault. A child is unable to read reality and extract shades of meaning, so the reality that identifies the tutor, or the abuser, as responsible for certain behaviours is not considered.

When grown up, victims state they were supposed to stop the thing from happening. It is their fault. Here we are dealing with the process of guilt explained beforehand by the client. Actually, it is a defence mechanism:… *"if I hadn't caused the problem, all this wouldn't have taken place…"*

One may ask, *"Why does all this go on?"*

It is because survivors are unable to experience the feeling of powerlessness related to death. The **death of many expectations.**

This is one of the many shades of that reality to deal with in psychotherapy. Another reason is that there is the wish, "I so wish it had never happened".

Unfortunately, besides there being no protection, in case of incest, parents sometimes identify them as the "provokers". This can come from the abuser, or the other parent.

A mother:... *"You know doctor ...sometimes I have the impression that it's my daughter* (not yet 3 years old) *who is a flirt..."* This mother had not asked herself why her daughter had such an abnormal behaviour (an acting out). A psychiatrist told her that the girl was dealing with her Oedipal fantasies... This child, three years old once said to her mummy: "when daddy puts his "pissy" here (touching her genitals) he hurts me...".

As I said before, some children are so needy of attention and care that they accept any form of contact included erotic touching. Sometimes the molestation produces pleasant feelings thus increasing guilt and confusion, because on one hand, the needy part is satisfied, and on the other, there is guilt about doing such things. In adolescence, when molestations have been going on since infancy, it may happen that the victim can find the strength to say, "That's enough", but the damage has been done.

Mary used to go to her friend's home after school (primary) because at her place nobody was home. Before meeting her friend, she was molested by her friend's father. This went on for many years. When in high school and she became interested in flirting with school- mates, she found the courage to stop the abusive relationship but had to realize that she could not bear any kind of physical contact and no effusions of love. Experienced reactions of disgust and refusal to have pleasant sensations... *"I feel that the disgust I had towards Loretta's father, remained on my skin..."*

During the therapeutic process, clients also connect with SHAME.

The person must come to terms with such feeling and with guilt. This is the only way through which it is possible to have access to the abused part rejected by the victim, and then be capable of living with oneself as a whole. The **sexual experience** is "cut out" from the Self but it must come back.

Sometimes children have particular behaviours that are the Signal of their uneasiness. This is what Robert says:

"…I remember that at the time when I was undergoing such things, my sister didn't want to go to bed at night and at the same time she would be overtaken by violent itching over her legs and would scratch herself until she was bleeding. Last week I told her I am coming here for a psychotherapy and mentioned my problems and asked her if she had gone through the same problems at the time she had all that itching stuff. She started crying and screaming to stop. She didn't want to know anything else, and wouldn't listen any longer. I fear she has gone through my same fate…"

Another important step in psychotherapy is processing LOSSES.

One must go through the pain for the losses mentioned before. Awareness emerges for the loss of the Essence of Childhood. The image and uprightness of a Parent is lost. In the case of incest, it is lost forever. He can no longer be relied on. He is a father who has been a Lover.

Of course, these aspects come up at the end when the most painful aspects have emerged and have been processed and accepted. The person must have gained a Personal Power and a functioning Actualizing Tendency before such concepts, so cruel, but so real, can be accepted and processed.

Nevertheless, this is **The Reality**: things have really gone this way.

On the contrary, if we do not stay in reality, we move in a schizophrenic reality: *I know that you know that I know but we cannot say…*

It all pertains to the mourning of losses and illusions. Often, refusal to get into these parts of the "black hole" is manifested with pain, rage and fear, so as… *"why me?...it's not fair…"*.

The victim must come to terms with the **limit of things** (the limit of omnipotence) which are part of our "Being in the World". The philosophical concept of "limits," is a very important aspect of the process. It must be experienced in order to be able to accept reality and attain the "psychological principle of reality" in the wholeness of its "Being"…

By means of a paradox effect or process, the dying, by yielding to this reality, enhances integration of the Self. It is a Redeemed Reality…

When I accept reality and give up insidiously refusing it, the wounded part, rejected, becomes part of the Self, as a Citizen of the World… There comes a change from a feeling of being shattered to a feeling of wholeness …this gives way to a period of "convalescence".

Special attention in the case of INCEST.

When it happens that the offender is a parent, it is very hard to accept the Construct of a "father-lover" because during the developing process, the child (and the therapist…) have interiorized the universal value of "taboo" into the Basic Personality. On one hand, there is the part that experienced violence and betrayal, on the other, the taboo feeling pertaining to the part of being a "citizen of the world," which prevails over the abused part.

The victim experiences the dramatic VIOLATION by the father, or mother, burdened with the interiorized taboo. It gives way to a dreadful rage for being "cheated". The survivor states, "It is impossible to share such feelings with others, except for those who have gone through the same fate". The trouble is that she herself is part of "the others". The victim is also one of "those who cannot understand" because what has happened is a taboo. She must become conscious of this "havoc" and understand that the incommunicability she/he is talking about is also "dwelling" in him/her, being a "citizen of the world". Sometimes the client shouts out: *you will never be able to understand me…*" but she/he also will not understand until the confusion dissolved.

The LAST STEP of the process, for all victims of sex abuse, consists of reaching the most painful aspect of the wound. THE ROOTS OF THE TRAUMA. In order to reach the deep fear, which is the "original experience" of the **"traumatic event", one must reach the experience of annihilation…** There where something dangerous took place. It is very hard to go through this point and call up the feelings, but helps the person to experience being **"VICTIM AND CO-PROTAGONIST".** In those moments, in that **"here and now" it is her/him** who was there. It is an experience that belongs to the victim's story. Yes, there is a victim, but before that, there is the "co-protagonist". The root/origin of the trauma is the **"sexual experiencing".** Emotions, erotic emotions, were, in spite of all, an experience, pleasant or disgusting or whatever. This is a point that a child too must go through in therapy (play therapy). It might be cruel, but before that, there is "being" a protagonist. That person **was there…**

"I have been in a place where not even angels dare to go…" This is where that Personal Construct, the soothing metaphor used as a veil over so much havoc, is used.

Only when the feeling of innocence is recovered, can the victim find citizenship in the world and again **be like others**. When the survivor takes back their "lost" innocence, giving acknowledgment to the "sexualized" part of the Self, the CIRCLE of the existential act IS CLOSED.

When all this work is carried out, the victim **"connects with something that goes deep inside, "transcends" the material Self of the "Being" and meets the humanity of EXISTING".**

It is in the finitude of being that the human sacrifice is accomplished. The individual regains a "spiritual" feeling that frees him/her from the "chains" of "Being".

Maslow describes this aspect as somewhat "spiritual" when in encounter groups one goes down to the depths of feelings enhancing a special communication between participants. It is of a "spiritual kind". The moment when energy moves at the same rhythm thus, "transcending" one's being and experiencing the "humanity of existing".

Being a protagonist

The co-protagonist is the PREY. Being a **"prey"**, affects the basic feeling of **"existing"**, crushing the victim deep in the world of existence. An "I – ME". Being a **"victim"**, describes the basic feeling of **"Being"**; the sense of "who one is in the world": "I –Thou". It is very hard to go through this point and call up feelings but it helps the person to experience being "VICTIM AND PROTAGONIST": in those moments, in that **"here and now" she/he** was there. An experience that belongs to her/his story. Before being a victim, there is "being a protagonist".

The prey and not a party to the event, according to Freudian theory (De Zulueta). In psychotherapy, I never found the Freudian fear of punishment, (punished by one parent because I desired the sex of the other one) but pain at betrayal and fear of being alone. Left at the mercy of the abuser and **his intentions,** and the paralyzing feeling of being deprived of any form of respect.

Guilt is not felt towards the enemy/mother about the contended father, but used to conceal the refusal of one's powerlessness and thus the acceptance of reality; that is:

- Failure to control the situation.

- Having to recognize that they "lost the game". This is a reality that differs from the Freudian theory.

When working in therapy with children, the metaphor of the "prey" is important to role-play and play it to the extreme of "BEING DEFEATED". Children also, receive help when they accept this reality.

Freddy: *the prince was fighting with his sword, and was killing everybody.*

Th.: *But at the end he was defeated.*

Freddy: *Nooooo!*

Th.: *Yes… also a prince can be defeated. He doesn't always win… but this doesn't mean he is no longer a hero…*

Freddy: (After a while) *…I'll think this over…*

The experience of being "victim" is something that comes "afterwards". It is important to strip away "that skin" too. Often victims say… "*I wanted to strip away my skin*". It is here where the "TO BE" of being takes place. The "I-Me" experience occurs "before" being a victim. Often when they talk about the event, they mention things as if they "were not there," as if those things happened to a "foreign" part of them, whereas the two parts "must" be integrated in order to repair the damage. On the contrary, their psychic world is withdrawn. The body is at the mercy of "existing" deprived of "experiencing", but the body holds the "signs" of the experience, blocked in a wasteland feeling, a feeling of being in ruins.

If the client can handle this piece of the "puzzle" and says that "this is the truth", those things were "experienced by ME", there is no "if this", "if that". Things went "this way". **I lost the game**. It is an unchangeable reality: it was "her" being there with all the baggage of *EROTIC EXPERIENCING*. At this point the "victim" disappears and *"you are there in the NAKEDNESS of your BEING…*Because **"this is the point from which everything started"**.

The person feels lighter, as if a burden had been taken away. There was something very heavy: **the burden of a denied experience**. Otherwise, there will be an everlasting "reiteration", a "short circuit". Trauma reiterates.

This process gives way to one thing and its opposite. At the end, there is no longer "if" … "but" … "maybe", but the dramatic "**EROTIC** EXPERIENCE". **The piece removed…**

I have already pointed out that there is not a "standardized" process. We must know the several aspects of the "being" involved in this specific event and know when to give "input" at the emotionally appropriate moment. I can state that deep in the black hole , there is mortification often confused with the feeling of shame which has to do with the I-THOU, whereas mortification has to do with the I-ME. Only when the victim gets into the feeling of *mortification of the being*, caused by non-respect, trampled on, there comes the reaction of **a wounded dignity.** Eventually, from the depths of this feeling springs **empowerment.**

The feeling of a "dignity", which is the "drive" for any kind of empowerment, is possible only when the victim has gone through the mourning of all aspects of abuse and accepts the losses suffered.

Last and not least, there is also pain for the impunity of the abuser, but when the survivor is able to forgive themselves and regain the wholeness of the Self, this pain is soothed. Accepting reality, accepting having lost the game, there is no need to forgive, there is only pure **REALITY.**

REALITY IS NEITHER RIGHT NOR WRONG BUT ... **"IS".**

If the trauma took place at an age when verbalization was hardly developed, it proves difficult to "re-visit" those places. Sometimes there are signals without story, but only feelings. We do not know where they are coming from.

For example, a client talks about an instinct to grab her father's penis when in the car alone with him. She has only fragments of memories, *"I remember going upstairs in a place I don't remember where. It was when I went on holidays with my father alone. Now and then, I have the sensation of a sour taste like sperm. I remember the afternoons when I used to go to bed with him... that's all..."*

Now her sexual life with her husband is very difficult... *"it is a terrible strain for me to let him touch me, but I do it because I know I cannot refuse it..."*

From a session:

A young boy living in a community for drug addicts committed suicide by hanging himself. My client, a young female staff member, is very upset: *"for the injuries, the millionth time he injured his body"* she says.

From what she says, it turns out that what her mind is fretting about is not the fact that he is dead. Death was not part of her worries, it was the "violence" he did to his body: *"he had already used violence to himself when he used to prick himself; violence for the low consideration of his body...”* she says again.

“His body no longer had a protector“, I replied to her.

“Yes” ... she replies.

I continue ... *“this also happens in* sexual abuse. (I gave this input, because she went through abuse in childhood) ...*It goes like,* “you can do what you like”, says the victim to the abuser ...I’m not there ...”

The client answers to my graft: ... *“and you let the body live the experience on its own...”* I continue... *the first violence came from the abuser but also from the part of yours that says ‘I’m not there”...*

She answers ... *“I did that to myself...”* Silence...After a long time she slowly comes back and continues ...*At that moment it is like being on top of the Himalaya... You are alone...*

She stops but I decide not to let her go and catch her emotion and I describe the scenery she gave me ...*There is the absence of somebody, and no one can hear you...and you haven’t the resources to do anything...*

She continues ... **“and a deadly terror comes up inside”**... Another shift from outside to her inside world.

Here it is clear that **in an experience of terror there is the loss of Self Power.**

I decided to try to use a graft because I was touched by the fact that she kept on going back with a feeling of terror, anguish and anger, to the **“violence”** *the boy had done to his body;* an extremely secondary aspect compared to his death. I first shared with her this odd point. I told her I was touched for her deep emotions concerning the ill- treated body. She understood why I was showing this to her. My responses and graft lead her down to “her” world of violence, fear and terror when abused in childhood.

Once I tried the graft, if she was not able to get into her story I would never had added on my own the piece she added to her own story.

The survivor’s cry:
“Please help me heal my wounds”.
The abuser’s cry:
“Please lead me out of worlds
that art not mine”.

12 The abuser

The following are considerations and theoretical analyses that need further research. The following analysis differs from the theory stemming from Freudian theory.

From a session
FIRST EXAMPLE: A MOTHER
A little girl, five years of age, was touching a baby in a pram. The girl's mother says to her, "*Watch out. Babies must not be touched…*" The girl keeps on touching… "*watch out or I'll spank you…*" The girl takes her hand off the baby, but then slowly goes back…and at this point there is a struggle between mother and child. Besides the baby's mother, there are other mothers, but nobody interferes. "*…If you do it again I'll pull down your knickers and spank you…*" The girl stretches out her hand and her mother grabs it. Starts pulling down her knickers and "at last" (I say) the little girl "reacts" and screams… *"Mummy please don't do it…"* and clings to her mother's legs. Nobody reacted, because I suppose all the adults were "allied" with the mother of this "spiteful" "domineering" little girl.

Sometimes children perceived as those who want to dominate and take over our power, are just striving to **exorcize fear and impotence** experienced and suffered owing to the adult's irrational conviction of having to do with a dominating child. **An child's inexistent challenge.**

The baby's mother (my client) could have done something, for example moving away with the pram… but …she was an **abusive**

mother...

In fact, she reported that she too was against that little girl: *"...I was in a rage and waiting for the moment when there would be blows and I would have enjoyed the scene..."*

I asked my client. *"Where was your inner little girl?"* – She answers: *"...she was there still...motionless, waiting for the blows to arrive...".* I continue. *"There was only the body of the girl that was going to be beaten. In that moment you had decided "not to be there"...-* She bursts into a desperate cry, comes over to me and clings to my legs...

Later she would say. *"I was crying for that little girl of mine who at that moment used to become just blows..."*

A few weeks before this session she recalled the following: *"...when brother and I used to hear mother tossing the pans around in the kitchen, fear began to rise. We couldn't understand what was going on since we were playing and not mucking around. Neither did we know how it was going to end up"...* (Silence...)...I ask her if it was scary ...she answers... *"when the blows came, there was no fear ....There were only blows and I used to "become" the blows...Then a pleasant feeling would arise because I used to sense her violence penetrate me* (It passed through the defence system). *I was powerless...a prisoner of her fury that wouldn't let go"...*Silence... - I say to her: *and you felt you were without anyone protecting you ... -* She continues - *and I felt my mother's pleasure in feeling so free to beat me...*

Here the two parts: victim and abuser mingle together. **Most likely it is here, in this space left open by the paralyzed psychical withdrawal that the "monster" (the abuser's aggressiveness) penetrates the victim's Self. The structure of Existence is shattered.**

During the session mentioned above, I used one of my grafts:

I felt I was deeply in empathy with her feelings. When this happens I try to "restore" reality of the "here and now" and I do it when I feel I'm "clasped" (I am her "buddy"!!) to the other person and the other is ready to go down deeper.

Th. ...*At that moment, you were her prisoner...*

Cl. ...*Yes... I was there alone... I only had to stay still...*

Th. ...*You were in a place where not even angels dare to go...*

Cl. ...*Yes... I was scared because I couldn't know how long the blows would go on or what would happen ...and I was alone at the mercy of her fury*

At last, she could cry for her loneliness and the dispossession of her personal power. Her cry was like a plaintive baby's cry.

This client, during her childhood and now a young mother, experiences erotic feelings when she is in the presence of infants who are left "unguarded": *...I smiled ...with a grimace ...I used to think... "now I can do what I like, I'm free to do whatever I want. The baby is alone, and has no protection...* 'She would masturbate herself or sexually molest the child. Now she says...*" the pleasant feeling coming from the fact that nobody was there and that the baby was unable to tell these things, was terribly strong...*

When her son wants something, also previously when he was a baby and was hungry, she has the feeling of him "dominating" her and pounces on him with all her rage. (Other parents also report this mechanism).

In her therapy, **when she connected with the relinquished part of herself,** she recovered **her** impotence, **her** loneliness, **her** ancient fear. She was able to see her son's fear and understood the damage she was reproducing.

These contents are likely to suggest that perversion sets in on processes of regression.

It seems that **the source** of both behaviours, (both the sexual and physical violence) is the removal of an experience *of terror* that **turns into eroticism or violence**... It is the terror of a person who is annihilated, prisoner of the other, "dismantled", without protection and without any fault... **"My parents were supposed to be there"** was the statement of an abused client.

In those moments, there is withdrawal of the psyche. The body is left at the mercy of an "existing" deprived of the "experiencing", but the body holds the signs/signals of the experience blocked in a sensation of devastation.

*"...violence can undermine and change the structure of "existing"...*says a client...*"this is the reason why we ask ourselves:" why have I got the right to exist?"...*

Thus, a **terror** that leads to murder:

Cl *....Oh God! What does she (the daughter) want?... I can't understand...and fear and terror are swelling up .... and if I make a mistake?...I panic... the baby keeps on crying...and I don't understand...I feel I am choking...I get into a fierce rage, because she is asking me something...*

Th. *...Have no tools...you can't find anything...*

Cl. *...Yes... and now what can I do?   I feel the void coming up...* She stops talking. I feel her terror. I see the violence in her eyes and send her an empathic feedback. In turn I say: *I feel there is fear…a paralyzing fear that turns into a "deadly feeling"* …I try to reply to her, as if I were her in that moment.

Cl. *…I understand why a mother can kill …because in order to stop the terror, I must eliminate the thing that is causing it. The baby turns into my monster".*

This client is a physical abuser.

SECOND EXAMPLE: A FATHER

"…When my daughter cries I get violent. A ferocious anger grows in me, I try to control it, but I burst out"… Helping the client to go into these feelings, he understands that when the girl cries, he does not understand what she might need. He gets scared because he feels incapable of dealing with what is going on. He also feels he has not the means… is overtaken by panic…and gets violent.

It seems that these people in such situations have **lost all frames of reference. There is a threatening "unknown"…**

In the first example the reason why terror may lead to an erotic perversion or to physical violence, may depend on the fact that the child is experiencing being alone, frail, at the mercy of a reality the adult is unable to cope with: it is dissociating. The **deadly feeling, denied** in the adult's childhood, is likely to lead towards an erotic world.

The proof comes from the field of sexual perversion where excitement and arousal arise by means of dangerous behaviours: hands and strings around one's neck, injuries or severe torture to the body and so on.

There are also war events that talk about this: People who are strangers to each other, happen to meet in situations of extreme danger and have sexual intercourse.

THE ANCESTRAL BEHAVIOUR FOR THE SAFEGUARDING OF THE SPECIES?

In the second case, (physical violence) the "threat" seems to come from the victim's "power":… *"she is challenging me"*… *"she wants to dominate me"*… *she is asking me for something, but I don't know how to manage it. The "unknown is threatening me".*

In the first case, the dominating perception of the other: Frail and left Alone. The denied ancient terror turns into Eros.

In the second case, the dominating perception: Strong and Dominating. The denied ancient terror into violence

It is most likely that **abusers' hidden terror and pain** have the "opportunity" of being experienced at the time when they are abusing others.

The question that arises could be the following: Are there two pains and two terrors that meet in that instant? The child's terror and the terror of the abuser's inner child. The question grows from the fact that abusers often say that after the abuse there is a deep depressive episode… But just a little after, the child is blamed (victim) because the abuser must preserve his "original" mechanism: denial. (The one of his inner child), and claim the innocence of his adult side…

The reason why he does this lies in the fact that he has never been able to accept reality. The two parts are still divided…

I hold the conviction that it is *terror,* dwelling in the **structure** of the *"Existing"* that produces the feeling of incapacity, lack of tools, impotence, being powerless, thus preventing the cognitive part to maintain a critical sense of reality, clearness of mind, thus a feeling of Confidence.

Such a ruin causes *another fear;* the one towards all that is external to the Self: panic and terror are responsible for abnormal behaviours of the *"Being".*

I will conclude these comments taken from a phenomenological lecture and needing further research, with a personal idea of mine.

In the abuser's "inner world", perversion does not have to do with "Power", but with **"Defeat"**.

It is **the rejection** of defeat in the process of "Being in Perversion" first, and **refusal** of "Being in Defeat," in the **acting out** "afterwards". The refusal of impotence: if I am impotent, it means I have LOST THE GAME, but I AM INNOCENT and HOLD ON TO MY BEING IN INNOCENCE. YOU ARE CHEATING ME.

It is an obsessive exorcizing of the feeling of being defeated…of having lost the game…thus a **cunning "cry"**: I will not give up… I want what I had the right to receive… because "I am innocent".

A piece of story by a client *(Written after a session)*

I am upset by the T.V report I saw last night about the "X" crime (a mother is charged with murdering her two year old son but claims she's innocent). *Struck with the brutality and the sudden and unexpected explosion of insane hatred.*

I go to my session all closed up inside, reticent and confused.

Maddalena tells me that it's the little inner- girl/victim that saw the service on television, she is upset and now, is "blocked with terror" (I understood this after 30 minutes, so I gave her my feedback. The outside world was talking to her about something concerning her "inside world". The outside world has something to do with her inside world: "her" past story of abuses).

Straight away I recall to my mind my mother's face in an explosion of rage and violence, her mouth wide open in a roar, foam coming out of her mouth, her crossed-looking eyes, at a distance of a millimetre from my face are staring into nothingness.

Not only was I frightened by her violence, but also by her insanity.

It was a fear that went beyond that step of tension/alertness/mistrust in which you are owing to the unknown next move. It was the terror and bewilderment in front of those eyes that were detached from the world. Blindness that could not see me, completely withdrawn into a dimension of madness, transfiguring the face of a mother I was not able to recognize anymore. Not even as an abuser with the awareness of being so.

The impression I have now, looking at mother X's face while she is answering very calm and quiet, to the journalist's questions, is the horror to know that she may have known, even for just a few seconds, the violent monster hidden behind normality and who, after showing up , goes back and hides silently in the darkness of the unknown. Nobody, except "you victim", (the client - the child) *noticed anything. Nobody, and she least of all, can even imagine its existence.*

At this point, I am touched with two things:

First, the unimaginable, the painful rejection of me as a mother, of the possibility of being a monster for my children.

Second, the desert of solitude in which I child/victim was left to die with terror.

In the session that followed, I made an incredible effort to remember why the week before I walked out of my session crying.

During these last weeks, I realized that, during my sessions, I end up so confused on what is coming up that I forget many pieces of the therapy.

This disorientation depends on the fact that at this specific moment of my process I am narrating with more voices, exactly two: that of the child/victim (see the terror above) and that of the adult abuser (see the guilt towards my children). Since these parts are not yet integrated, but can only co-exist in a new consciousness I have achieved, I must stay in this split in order to give voice to them. It is this split that is causing my disorientation.

On the other hand I am not ready to see the experiences of a third part, that of me victim/adult/abuser, so this voice is not yet making itself heard… it still needs to hide…

My conclusion is that the **DRIVE** to violence is not the need of Power, but **the need to defeat DEFEATEDNESS**.

The cry of the inner-child is "I shall never give up because I am innocent…and I have the right to be given what I am craving for. From a "dynamic point of view," what happened? I think that the split consists of the fact that "pain and terror" are rejected whereas "claimed innocence" goes to the cognitive level.

Later, there is an "adult" unable to "give up" the dream, and take care of their " inner child" because they are unable to connect with their underlying feelings of violence, pain, terror and sorrow suffered in childhood, which have to do with **"not being attended to"**, according to the "sacred values" that a caregiver should always uphold, and of **"being violated"**. This is a burden added to the prior **"I am innocent"**.

In violent people, there is always the hidden/rejected "innocent inner-begging child", in all patterns of interaction. That is why battered women say, "he looks so nice, so sweet"… The innocent, defeated, stubborn child who is always asking, but simultaneously expecting the blows… and there goes the "fear-attack" reaction towards the mysterious enemy (the victim).

I started this book with a letter and shall end it with a letter. This letter is mine. A letter I wrote, but obviously never delivered, to a young client with a destructive personality.

My dear frightened friend,
Your distance, the one you are keeping between me and you, I recognized the first time you entered my studio. And I have managed to respect it every moment, except when I have had to seize that instant in order to throw a small stone into

the pond, taking the risk, so that you may see, for an instant, what lies just below the surface, hoping it will not hurt you too much.

When I started this profession, a job suggested to me by a university dean, I didn't imagine the amount of pain and sorrow I was to hold, rather than listen to. Maybe it is owing to the willingness I undoubtedly developed by means of the sorrow I personally suffered , so don't worry, even though I feel and contain it, it does not overcome me, because the years of psychotherapy I myself went through have healed my wounds, so I am not overwhelmed. I confess, honestly, that sometimes, certain pains make me feel the desire to find, at the end of the day, enfolding arms to help me drain "my" sorrow for others' sufferance.

So as you see I am not a "super-woman!" All this enables me not to keep away from the other's sorrow, because I keep it separated from mine. Of course, I am sorry, and I feel powerless "staying" with the pain and sorrow the person is suffering and bearing, in a "struggle" that is sometimes too heavy for his/her shoulders ... but this is what has to be done.

Thanks for the compliment saying you liked me straight away ... even though you are saying it with fear. When you entered my studio I understood that you were "adorable", bad-tempered ... yes bad-tempered... but under the skin there is a sweet lad, lonely, craving for warmth and love ... unfortunately a "kind of warmth and love" that I can't give you. You can perceive, as you say, what it consists of, but not I nor anyone else, are your mother or father, the only ones who were supposed to give what you are searching for.

Yes, I know, my silence kills, but I also know, by experience, that with time, it makes you feel free, to stay and do what you like ... and that is where love comes, helping heal the wounds. It "only" helps, because you are the one who has to do the work, and it is the experience of this silence that makes you sense that I shall never betray you. You are free to keep an eye on me, under control. It doesn't upset me and, as you say, I don't have to conceal anything.

I don't know if I am impenetrable ... certainly I am so in those moments when I am extremely attentive listening and seizing those points or moments when feedback is precious or even risky. Sometimes it is important to "seize the moment". Yes, it's true, and I am writing it with a smile, I personally disappear, but my eyes remain ... and there you can find all you need. And when you see I am not there, do take or find the courage to lift up your glance and look into my eyes ... and there, there is not a void and there you shall not lose yourself. You say you are scared to look into my eyes, because you do not want to grasp my warmth, thus feel your violence that protects your unbearable, still hidden pain and the terror of your wounds.

Yes, my dear friend, you are right again on this: the void howls ... the empty *screaming of the void. A void that wants filling. But: void is filled only with its own void: the **I-ME** and you have lost the game: the **I-THOU***

A loving hug

**enfold your inner child
in your loving arms.
Tell your child
the game is lost.
Then move on to
the Ocean of Life
The therapist's cry.**

*Now that you're out there
on your own
remember that what
is real and what we dream
is love alone.
"beautiful that way". Noa*

Part 3

Presentation at the Carl Rogers
Annual Conference 2019

13 San Diego

In 2019 at the annual conference held in San Diego, I made a presentation pointing out the validity of the client centred approach in tune with the present theories in quantum physics - neurosciences and modern psychology, and how spiritualism "fits" in Person-Centred Therapy

Part 1: Lecture
Part 2: Spiritualism in Rogerian Therapy

PERSON CENTRED THERAPY AND RESEARCH FOR MEANING AND SELF-TRANSCENDENT LOVE IDENTITY IN PSYCHOLOGICAL HEALTH

ABSTRACT

Humans are given birth into the world with all their/our inborn potentialities and singularity. It is an "atom/seed" that would give life to a personality in harmony with the environment, should there not be a distortion of their/our Actualizing Tendency.

These aspects are reviewed through a phenomenological interpretation and compared with the new frontiers in the scientific world of physics.

THIS LECTURE WANTS TO BE MY HOMAGE TO CARL ROGERS; WHO, MANY YEARS AGO, WITH THE HUMILITY AND HUMANITY THAT DISTINGUISHED HIM, PLANTED THE SEEDS THAT NOW ARE YIELDING THEIR FRUITS.

During these years of experience in Person Centred Therapy based on client's experiential world and SUBJECTIVE way of being, I carried out a careful study of the person's phenomenal world. At the same time, my attention was drawn also towards other scientific fields such as physics, biology and neurosciences that are advancing in knowledge through new discoveries.

This gave me the opportunity to move beyond phenomenology and reach the "valley" of quantum physics. Here I could correlate my studies in the phenomenal world, WITH QUANTUM PHYSICS which I *have clearly* explained in my book on the Short-Circuit in child sexual abuse.

My studies can prove that the non-directive approach is in line with "modern psychology" which draws parallels with modern physics on one side while with classic Indian philosophy dating back to centuries before Christ on the other.

I owe much to neurosciences, mainly to professor Stephen Porges, who I met in Milan, for discovering the importance of the "role" of emotions and feelings in our behaviours. But, this is not enough. As Ervin Laszlo (2014) holds, **"there *is* an *'underlying' eternal nonlocal* nature** *of the events"*. Transferred to psychotherapy, it means that there is an 'underlying' subjective 'Story' of every existential act or action.

AS FAR AS I KNOW, AT PRESENT ONLY CLIENT CENTRED APPROACH CAN REACH THESE DEPTHS, BECAUSE THE "RAILWAY" TO THOSE AREAS IS THE CLIENT'S SUBJECTIVITY AND THE THERAPIST'S CLOSE EMPATHY WITH THE CLIENT'S CONGRUENCY AND INCONGRUENCY

Why am I sure that Carl Rogers is a forerunner of modern Psychotherapy?

Rogers initiated his career and a personal psychoanalysis in tune with those times, but very soon, he moved towards a non-directive approach. Those were the years of positivistic philosophy that gave life to: theoretical – structural psychology and theoretical frames of reference. Later, positivism evolved to existential philosophy focusing on subjective experience, emotions, deep feeling and at present it is evolving toward a widespread feeling of **compassion and cosmic love.** A field now coming to interest even modern physicists.

I understand and feel the refusal by psychoanalysts and behaviourists, who are locked and encased in their cardinal thoughts: I suggest, they should make attempts to dismantle their lines of thought, but this is evolution that would be a revolution!

Physicists, who have to do with "matter" and elements of the universe, reached this step before us. They believe there is a network of **perfect harmony and respect** embracing the **whole universe.** Anyhow, it is comprehensible: They deal with elements of the UNIVERSE of which we are a "grain of sand".

Never the less psychologists can walk in parallel with them if endowed with **"Cosmic Love" and "Respect",** because Cosmic Energy is an entanglement of harmony and respect and we are part of that energy.

As regards harmony and respect, I always remember the **"black hole"** IN THE UNIVERSE, which is an icon of regard and respect in the physical world AND CLIENT CENTRED THERAPY IS AN ICON OF REGARD AND RESPECT IN the psychological world.

Person centred approach, which moves in troubled waters, sometimes delving into the world of the client's "black holes", can go *deep down* to the *roots* of distorted actualizing tendency and at the same time *rise* to the *peaks* of **compassion and cosmic love.** My book on child sexual abuse, clearly explains the process.

PCA is a process that works with the client's experiencing in the **"here and now"** and at the same time with the **story of the past**, bringing a change in one's emotional world and behavioural patterns, because it goes down and seeks out the source of the problems where we find the *"primary fears and dysfunctional behaviours of our inner child".* Neuroscience also holds that special exercises can heal a trauma, but only a psychotherapy can heal the wounds at their roots.

Many years ago, Carl Rogers, although unaware, was trying to prove that PCA is a quantum process. But, physics, psychology and biology, at that time, were working separately and Rogers did not know he was a forerunner in "modern psychology".

Now the time has come to take a leap and travel with quantum theory. Where are we in parallel with physics? Here are some principles:

--- PCA: I am the therapist and at the same time, I am the client: Empathy.

--- PHY: A subatomic particle can be "**here**" but *also* "**there**" at the same time: Non- locality

--- PCA: The process consists in working at the surface (present) and at the same time walking upon an underlying experience of the past.

--- PHY: A single part can affect the Whole, but the whole can influence the underlying world: Akasha Field

--- PCA: The approach moves toward the *ocean* of life and at the same time, moves back to the source *(roots)* of live. The two ends meet.

--- PHY: From the depths of *subatomic world* to the *peaks* of Cosmic Love.

--- PCA: Our psychotherapy goes to the depths of the client's phenomenal world, and at these DEPTHS, meets the BEGENNING and embraces the "whole network" of the **Being.**

--- PHY: The Gravitational **Wave**

WHAT HAPPENS IN OUR PROCESS?

At the beginning, the process deals mainly at "the high levels". At the surface the client deals in the worlds of the *"I –Thou"*. Emotions and feelings are mainly "reactive". Later, level after level the process moves deeper down TO THE PRIMARY PHENOMENAL WORLD where pain, wounds, losses, sorrow, fear, become clearer and consciously experienced. We are mainly in the realm of the *"I – Me"*. Healing is on the way. HERE THE WOUNDS ARE BLEEDING.

At a deeper level: the very roots of the "tree of life" there is a world of silence, darkness, anguish, bitterness, **SOLITUDE.** Sometimes there is a tough stubbornness: it is the soldier, standing at the door of the cave! The person is no longer in a dialogue between I-Thou or I-Me but with a *"Me"*: me and myself. Me and the door: *"I don't know what is behind the door. It is dark… a haunted place. As far as I use control I hold the game, Control is my only standpoint. Behind the door I have nothing…".* This state of being is highly present in adults abused (ill-treatments) in childhood and in destructive personalities. Why? They had to **bury** far down, deny anguish, fear and loneliness, in order to survive and avoid psychic disintegration. HERE WE ARE IN THE FIELDS OF BLACK HOLES (Here there are Short-Circuits) I found black holes in child sex abuse and in violent personalities.

IN this dimension, THE WORK GETS HARD: WE ARE IN

THE BLACK HOLE- ZONE. HERE WOUNDS HAVE BEEN FORESAKEN and don't bleed. It is the "not-me" explained by the psychiatrist H.S: Sullivan. The interaction client-therapist changes: It is a work of "confrontation" and "congruency" between client (adult part) and therapist (the wise cricket). There is pain and fear on one side (client) and "Reality" on the other (therapist). One of the two must "give up": actually, it is a duel between two parts of the client. There is the ***"therapist-caregiver"*** containing the inner-child (wounded part) and at the same time keeping the client stuck to reality: ***"The game is lost, my dear".*** On the other side, the ***"client-adult"*** is holding on to the ***"sense of Justice"*** and will not give up the game. This means that at higher levels, life is still sustainable with its strategies and behavioural patterns.

Here the therapist makes use of: pieces of the puzzle singled out by the client during the process and congruency with reality which, at the moment, can be pointed out only by the therapist.

QUANTUM PHYSICS DESCRIBES THIS AS A DANCE BETWEEN PARTICLES. YES! A dance between pieces of our puzzle of life! A PLACE WHERE MATHEMATICAL LAWS ARE NO LONGER PART OF THE GAME, BUT AT THE END, THE OUTCOME IS **A HARMONY WITH THE WHOLE.**

Explained in terms of an "experiential paradigm", the client is still holding on to the *dream of the "innocent": (what I want was to be given to me: the sacred need of a child)* though paying the price of frustrations and failures and though being conscious that nobody else can give him/her the "not given".

The dream is a "felt meaning" underlying the **"void"** of the not given (A   reality) and **"wounds"** (the experience of ill-treatments).The difficulty to relinquish the dream, can be explained in terms of an **underlying fear** to "let go, since when this ultimate tie/string is cut, the door is opened, and it means being totally alone in the world and with the "not me". Something like being launched into the world when we are born. *"If I let go, says a client, I must give up justice and this means I am defeated… and it is not fair; this is against nature".* ***Dignity*** has not yet reached the level that gives rise to a "switch over" to the feeling of "self-care". It is the ultimate cut of an umbilical cord. How can this be? The **Solitude** of the inner child who, behind the door, ***"pure and innocent", holding on to his "DREAM"*** (the unsatisfied need) is still there, left on its own, at the mercy of the unknown and it is the **string** fueling the strategies. But, the adult part is **still** claiming justice and the inner child is **still** waiting to be cared for.

These clients are in a world of the NOT-ME. Wounds do not bleed; they were silenced/frozen, from the very beginning: This is what triggers VIOLENCE. In other words, in between the world of **"Being"** and the underlying frozen world of the **"not me"**, stays "Violence"…in front of a **DOOR"**. (Don't you dare come in… in there, there is too much pain –fear and solitude)

Here, in this world, **darkness, hatred, demons** are still dwelling, the adult part is alone, in front of the door: it becomes a duel between the two: The adult and the door. From the research I have been carrying out as regards destructive personalities and psychotherapy with them, I noticed that at this point the players/dancers are two. One is the client: complaining and fighting against reality. The other is the therapist: answering and adding, new pieces of reality, but always in congruency and at the client's step. Slowly, through the world of feelings and of being and mourning, the client puts pieces together. The therapist's role slows down getting more silent. At the end, there is only ONE dancer: the client… alone… with his solitude. It's a world that has been silenced, a world in darkness where there has always been a silent plaintive cry. It is the "inner child" rolled up in solitude, pain and fear. *It is here my dear, where you must get back in order to recover your pure and innocent* **part** and in your child you shall discover your true *"Essence"*. Little by little, after recollecting all those painful moments and giving voice to the innocent complaints calling for justice, in accordance with physics, **at point "Zero"** energy shall turn into **purity;** *exactly there where the damage had origin.* It's a paradox, but I noticed that these people, at the very bottom, are bestowed with a pure and innocent soul: the soul of an innocent child.

This aspect is visible in Nature: nature regenerates life on life-long barren land and in Physics: the Akasha Field: particles hold the memory. As regards us: violence fades away and gives place, or, gives life to purity and innocence. Purity and innocence are invisible "elements" that hold memory. (the pure-innocent- frozen part of the Self).

What is all this about?

Shortly, this is the point:

Frank maintains: **on one side *there is my innocence. Innocence pertains to nature: It is natural that a child claims certain needs; it's the child's right, but the child is abused.* **On the other side,** *I am defeated, but it is not natural: what happened is against nature. And, if I give up, it is against nature.*

Yes! I reply. You are right, but in between these two laws, there is **REALITY** ***and you cannot change it***....*somebody hurt you*...

**The same thing happened with a sexually abused child: Jacky six years old. In a session he is playing with a sword and shouting: *"Now I am going to kill everybody with my sword".*

Th: *"You are a hero because you have been in a place where not even angels dare to go, but you have lost the game".*

Jacky: *"Nooooo"*....

Th. *plaintively* ... *"This is what happened, and sometimes also heroes lose the game. Nevertheless they remain heroes"*... Silence... (he is thinking). Then says".

Jacky: *"I shall think about this."*

After many years, I met him for some information concerning his work. At a certain point, he said: *"Sometimes we must accept to lose the game..."* Our eyes met... we knew what we were talking about...

Now I would like to go beyond the border, transcend the **"way of being"** and join the theoretical model concerning **"humanity of being"**. Being in tune with the "Whole": The dimension where there are values having to do with consciousness and evolution. As Fritjof Capra and Goswami state: *"once a society of minds recognizes its shared "collective identity", Selfishness, Cruelty, Suppression of others, are no longer viable survival modes".*

Can PCA attain these **peaks**? Yes.

The therapeutic process "ends" where or when one accepts Reality of one's story laying at the source (the roots of the tree of life). From there on, another Real /Authentic story will take place: It is the **Actualizing Tendency** that embraces philosophy and the world of Eastern Mystics, ***in tune*** with modern physics. That means to enter the dimension of ***"being a whole"*** where in a world of compassion there is no judgement, no prejudice. There is no longer an I-Thou, but only: **"One Is"**. It is there, where we meet our "enemy" who, no longer, is such for us. Here on one end the ***enemy*** on the other there is ***compassion***... where the two ends meet... (the innocent and the enemy) and beyond which, there is ***"Cosmic Love"***. In other words, we reach the peak of harmony and Self-actualization. (Laszlo). "At the end you shall thank your enemy and love your story. This is the title of my book on psychotherapy explaining all the long process **from the depths of a crying soul to the peaks of compassion and harmony.** This principle is the auspicious of the psychologist and anthropologist Vamik Volkan author of "Killing in the name of identity".

I would like to focus on the human/spiritual dimension which in our days is mentioned in physics - a long time ago - in philosophy by Maslow, - in psychology by Rogers and at present *even* by neurosciences: It is the dimension where one feels to be in a *"whole" with the "other"* on a human/spiritual level. From a scientific point of view, I am referring to a cosmic energy, an embracement with the whole; a gravitational wave. At the end of his life, Stephen Hawking in his studies states: *"I have reached the subatomic level, but underlying these particles, there is still something "mysterious":* The gravitational wave is an intelligent web of cosmic interconnections, where each part is entangled and affects the whole.The whole in turn, affects each part in a perfection of harmony and respect. (Akasha field). **It is the "ultimate" level,** that connects us to the universe, in a symphony of cosmic love and consciousness.

Akasha field is a particle that generates – regenerates – interconnects – holds memory.

ALL OUR PSYCHOTHERAPY MOVES IN A NON-DIRECTIVE APPROACH – A SUBJECTIVE EXPERIENC THAT LEADS THE CLIENT TO BEHAVE ACCORDING TO ONES ACTUALIZING TENDENCY: THE "ORGANISMIC SELF". AN APPROACH TO LIFE THAT HAS ITS LAWS EMBUED WITH HARMONY –PEACE – RESPECT: THE SAME LAWS OF THE UNIVERSE THAT ARE BEYOND RULES AND MATHEMATICS.

Gregory Bateson says:

The infinitely high

The depths of waters

The extreme and challenging complexity

of the multicellular

The apparent simplicity toward the unicellular

are all extreme elements of a unique equilibrium.

I AM PROUD TO STATE TODAY THAT **CARL ROGERS' PHILOSOPHY** HAS ALWAYS BEEN IN TUNE WITH THESE

NEW ASPECTS.

Here is a statement by psychologist SPINELLI, Richmond College, London. Exploration of the components and structures of subjective experience, even though subjective, nevertheless, in spite of all kinds of subjective experience, we all arrive at "unique interpretations" of our experience owing to biological, cultural, social aspects and according to me, owing to the most important universal constructs and values that unite us all to a Cosmic Design/Structure

REFERENCES:

Al-Khalili J. and Mc Fadden J. (2015). *Life on the Edge. The coming of Age of Quantum Biology*. Ed. Weidenfeld & Nicolson Ltd. London.

Boncinelli E. (1999). *Il Cervello, la mente e l'anima*. Ed. A. Mondadori Milano.

Capra J. (1975). *The TAO of Physics*. Ed. Shambhala Publications.

Citro M. (2011). *The Basic Code of the Universe*. Ed. Park Street Press. Vermont.

Laszlo E. (2014). *The Self-Actualizing Cosmos*. Ed. Inner Traditions. Vermont.

Goswami A. (2000). *A Quantum Physicist's Guide to Enlightenment*. Ed. Theosophical Publishing House. Wheaton.

Mindell A. (2912*). Quantum Mind. The Edge between Physics and Psychology*. Ed Deep Democracy Exchange. Oregon USA.

Nelson A.D. (2015). *Origins of consciousness*. Ed. Metarising Books. Nothingham. England.

Porges S.W. (2011). *The Polyvagal Theory. Neurophysiological foundations of emotions, communications and Self-regulation*. Ed. Norton.

Spinelli E. (1989). *An Introduction to Phenomenological Psychology*. Ed. Sage Publications. London

SULLIVAN H.S. (1972) The Interpersonal Theory of Psychiatry. W.W. Norton Company. Inc, New York.

Hawking S. (1998) *A Brief History of Time*. Ed. A Bantan Book. New York.

Siddhartha M. (2016). *The Gene*. Ed. Penguin Random House. India.

Volkan V. (2006). *Killing in the name of Identity*. Ed. Pitchstone Publishing Virginia.

SPIRITUALISM IN CLIENT CENTRED APPROACH

When is it experienced? At the roots of the tree of life when empathy, the Golden Invisible Thread turns into spirituality.

The pathway leading to spirituality is empathy. I believe that this is the narrow pathway, because when I deal with very painful situations, such as in destructive personalities, and am totally in empathy with the client, far down the roots of life, I realize at the end of the session, that for some moments I was no longer myself, but in a total empathy with the clients feelings, sometimes like an "identification"- a "channeling" with the other, but with a small part of myself holding on to the reality of his story. Here it is: "Yes, I respect your congruency with being innocent, but there is **only One Truth:** you have lost the game – you have been defeated even though being innocent. *Congruency with this reality is a special feeling,* something "spiritual": loss-pain- despair - compassion- grief- lovingness. Hand in hand, the person is lead from darkness to the light where respect and cosmic love are dwelling.

From a neurological point of view, the ***"mirror neurons"*** are the main workers in a work of "confrontation". I feel what he is feeling, but I am also feeling- giving voice to the "drama" of reality: a ***low sobbing cry*** of loss that, somehow, reaches the client because: my empathy "with reality" and with the "dramatic feeling" that he is experiencing, are in synergy. The moment when he will feel what I am feeling, it will become his. This work with children age 3 -4 and with autistic children gives its fruits. Hugging them and being in synergy with their anger or despair and my sorrow and lovingness and "containing" them in ***"their state of being"*** but **ALSO** *adding* ***"reality":*** *"it is not possible my dear".* Somehow, the child's "inside congruency" turns into congruency with the "outside reality" and they calm down.

HOW come?

**It is the: "let things go" of spiritualism.

**Here: Compassion (for Reality) – Respect (the child's need and cry) – Lovingness – are working in synergy.

**The OUTCOME is: "I let go the need"…

Unfortunately, this does not happen with our clients; it takes a long time before letting go and thus, "giving up". *Letting go **"the need"*** is the; *let things go* of **"spiritualism"**. In these moments, the "two actors" become A Whole with the universe. Anger or despair give place to compassion and respect. As time goes on, these two feelings, give way to a spiritual wisdom, which has nothing to do with religion. It is simply "another way of being".

The "material" way of being has to do with "outside world". The "spiritual" way of being, transcending the material things has to do with one's "interiority"…How come?... Our threads are cleaned from all what is "darkness" and a "golden light appears".… **"LILLIES GROW FROM MUD"**…

Rogers gave me the colours: empathy – unconditional positive regard – respect – responsibility – personal power and I painted some pictures: dream – strawberry ice cream – uncompleted existential act – many funerals. Eastern philosophy gives me intuitions and physics turns them into numbers.

travel.

The author

Born in Australia. Graduated in Psychology at University of Padova – Italy. Four years at the Facilitator Development Institute in Rome where I specialized in Rogerian Therapy.

My teachers and tutors were Carl Rogers, Chuck Devonshire, George De Rita, Nat Ruskin, John Wood.

During the four years in Rome, my tutor was Chuck Devonshire to whom I owe a great deal for his sensitivity and great capacity to convey the "non-directive" approach and the fundamental concepts of Person-Centred Therapy. These professors come from the Centre for The Study of The Person University at La Jolla in San Diego, California.

For four more years, I attended a supervision group conducted by Chuck Devonshire, treasuring a great deal of experience firstly with him and later with George De Rita. In my profession I was able to get hold of those "threads" that lay deep within the person's history and that "desperately" surface from the depths and become protagonists of our way of being ("the distorted actualizing tendency"). From this experience comes my book of poems: "A psychotherapy?...No... A lifetime...". It is a collection of poems written by a client and is the witness that there is a pathway in the therapeutic process. How long and painful is the road to travel.

For many years, I have been professor for Clinical Sexology at the Centro Italiano di Sessuologia in collaboration with the Clinical Sexology Service at the department of Psychology University of Bologna.

For ten years, I taught sex education in secondary schools and later wrote a book: "The voyage of our sexual growth".

I have written works on sexual topics for scientific reviews.

With this book on psychotherapy, I am here with all the limits that I realize may emerge, but with the hope that someone will take them and use them in order to move forward with a scientific "hand" in the phenomenal "Being in the World".

The last chapter is an attempt to give some theoretical evidence as regards child abuse. For this piece of work my thanks goes to Mariagnese Cheli, responsible for the "Centre against child abuse" of the Azienda Sanitaria of Bologna.

Read *A Psychotherapy? No... A Lifetime...*

Sometimes the therapeutic journey brings up a strong need to "fix" its most significant stages. So it happens that the person discovers a poetic vein in speaking and narrating. It's owing to this, that a client was able to track a pathway, to write a story of sorrow and of memories, nice and unpleasant; that the protagonist of the therapeutic process caught in her memory, slowly, slowly. And equally slowly, slowly she shaped the emerging figures in the fog with the aid of her psychotherapist. This piece of work shall lead the reader into the secrets of a therapy that turns out to be the research of the "true" story of the childhood of everyone of us. Each poem testifies how difficult it is to recall the past, to rebuild it through the renewal of emotions, anguish, experienced and concealed, until you find their sense by means of a crude, maybe cruel rereading of reality. It's as if we have many pieces of a puzzle of which we have lost the picture.

Read *Short-Circuit and betrayal in child sexual abuse*

The book describes a research in the field of child sex abuse. The intent is to point out specific aspects which will lead to a complete psychological recovery from trauma using the "Experiential Model" and moving back to the roots of the traumatic experience. The fact fostering a "total healing" is the individuation of the uncompleted "existential act", interrupted at the moment of the "molesting act". The specific aspect has to do with a "specific need" in the victim's story. The Rogerian approach is appropriate for the client to get in touch with the world of emotions and *go deep down* to parts of the Self that lead to the "black hole": the root bearing the experience of illusions - betrayal - defeat. At the same time it *leads up to the peak* of compassion and cosmic love. Thence, there, there it's gonna be another *"long walk home"*.

Bibliography

Buber M. I and Thou. Amazon.it

Courtois C.A. Healing the incest wounds in adults. Ed: Sage Publications London 1999

De Zulueta From Pain to Violence Amazon.it

Eliot T.S. The waste land and other poems. Ed. Faber and Faber. London 1999

Kohut H. Releasing the Self. Amazon.it

Maslow A. Towards a psychology of Being. Amazon.it

Miller A. The drama of the gifted child. Amazon.

Rogers C. Person Centered Counseling Amazon.it

Rogers - Kingest Person Centered therapy Amazon.it

Rogers C. Personal Power: Strength and its Revolutionary impact Amazon.it

Sartre J.P. Sartre e la realitè Humaine. Editions Seghers, Paris 1970

Spinelli E. The Interpreted World Sage Publications London 1989